GOOD CHARACTER

GOOD CHARACTER
A Comprehensive Guide to Manners and Morals in Islam

Musa Kazım Gülçür

Translated by Jessica Özalp

TUGHRA
BOOKS

New Jersey

Published by Tughra Books
335 Clifton Ave.
Clifton, New Jersey, 07011, USA

www.tughrabooks.com

Library of Congress Cataloging-in-Publication Data

Gulcur, Musa Kazim.
 [Adab-i muaseret. English]
 Good character : a comprehensive guide to manners and morals in Islam /
 Musa Kazim Gulcur ; translated by Jessica Ozalp.
   p. cm.
 Includes bibliographical references and index.
 ISBN 978-1-59784-134-4 (pbk.)
 1. Islamic etiquette. 2. Islamic ethics. 3. Muslims--Conduct of life. I. Ozalp,
Jessica. II. Title.
 BJ2019.5.I8G8513 2009
 297.5--dc22
                                                                        2008055623

CONTENTS

FOREWORD

The Islamic term used for a person's good character and breeding is *adab* (for which there is no single corresponding equivalent in English). Being a critical element of the Islamic ethos, *adab* refers to a comprehensive code of conduct: the concepts of decency, propriety, politeness, reverence, good manners, and good education and upbringing reflect various aspects of the rich Islamic term *adab*.

A person who has attained *adab* is one whose spirit has been shaped in accordance with the principles of religion until these principles have become part of their nature. In the larger sense, it also means such a person has a spirit which is permanently unified with the "Way," the path of right living. Accordingly, religion denotes not only spiritual beliefs, but a complete way of life—a path and a set of principles by which to live.

Adab, at the same time, refers to the attainment of the awareness that one is constantly dependent on and in the presence of God, Who sees everything; the result is that one acts with such awareness at all times.

More specifically, as an Islamic term, *adab* consists of observing the practices of Prophet Muhammad, peace and blessings be upon him, that is, the Sunna; *adab* is to do as he did in both the obligatory practices of Islam and the non-obligatory matters.

The following wise words were once said about the concept of *adab* that encompasses all these meanings: "*Adab* is a person's eternal clothing. A person with no *adab* is as though undressed," and "*Adab* is a crown from the Divine Light. Wear this crown and secure yourself from every calamity."

Adab is like a spiritual garment that protects the wearer from harm and misfortune. If you want to be saved from misfortune you should strive to have great *adab*. With *adab* one will have the knowledge of one's true self; but without *adab*, even knowledge will never make a person erudite. Accordingly, a person with no *adab* can never be considered to be wise, no matter how many tomes they may have memorized. In other words, a person only has true knowledge if they attain *adab* and without *adab* all learning will prove futile. For, as Yunus Emre, the famous Sufi poet of Anatolia, (1238–1320) said:

> Knowledge is to be enlightened,
> To be enlightened is to know one's self.
> If you do not know who you are
> What good can book-learning do?

The one who best embodied this *adab* is Prophet Muhammad, peace and blessings be upon him. In both word and deed he always manifested the highest degree of *adab*. One of the greatest and closest Companions of the Prophet, Abu Bakr, once asked him, "O Messenger of God, who gave you this *adab*?" He answered, "My Lord raised me and gave me the best *adab*."

After the death of the Prophet, his wife Aisha, the daughter of Abu Bakr, was asked, "What were the character and morals of God's Messenger?" She replied with a question, "Have you not read the Qur'an?" They said, "Yes." Upon this she said, "His character was the Qur'an."

Since his moral training came directly from God, all those who wish to learn *adab* should look to the Messenger of God as the standard for comparison; he is the paragon of *adab*.

The Almighty created Prophet Muhammad, peace and blessings be upon him, with an *adab* that represents an ideal for all humanity to aspire to. This was what gave him the ability to bear the heavy responsibility of being a Prophet. In this way he was created with a distinctive morality and etiquette which made him a perfect example for us.

During the youth of the Prophet the Ka'ba was being repaired and he was involved. Indeed, throughout his life the Prophet was always to be found wherever good works were being carried out. While carrying stones to use in the rebuilding of the Ka'ba, his uncle Abbas placed the skirt of his garment over his shoulders to cushion them under the heavy load. As Muhammad's shoulders were becoming bruised he suggested that his nephew do the same. To do this would have meant that his knees would have been exposed. When Muhammad, peace and blessings be upon him, started to follow this suggestion, before he could remove his outer garment an angel suddenly appeared before him. He fell to the ground in great fear. Thus, even before he was raised as a Prophet, Muhammad, peace and blessings be upon him, was always protected from doing wrong.

These are events from before Muhammad, peace and blessings be upon him, was entrusted with Prophethood. God Almighty did not allow him to stray at any stage of his life. This is an exceptional distinction that belongs solely to being a Messenger of God.

How could it be otherwise for him? When the Prophet was still a child, his chest was opened and angels removed the spot of Satan from there, discarding it. This black spot, which exists in every human and which Satan uses as a target for his arrows, did not exist in the Messenger after that day. Yes, Satan, who whispers into hearts and runs through our very veins, could not come near this man. Prophet Muhammad, peace and blessings be upon him, was indeed an extraordinary person.

In the same way that he was protected in early life from committing sins, so too was he protected later by God. He lived as cleanly and purely as on the day he was born. From the first to the last day of his life, God's Messenger was the very embodiment and manifestation of *adab*.

The Prophet's *adab* encompassed every aspect of life. In every situation he practiced *adab*. When there was an injustice, the Prophet would never rest until he had righted the wrong. At these times he had the strength of a lion. Yet, the same man would never so much as frown with displeasure, much less act in defense or revenge, even when the greatest of injustices were carried out against him personally. Such is the behavior required by true *adab*.

Although the Companions of the Prophet were among the purest of people, one of them, who had not yet thrown off the influence of his previous life, once became agitated and grabbed the Messenger by the collar, demanding his rights. His grip was so tight that the collar left marks on the Prophet's neck. Instead of retaliating for this behavior, the Prophet responded with a smile and said "Give this man what he has asked for," and let the matter go at that. Thus we can perceive his forbearing kindness and immense tolerance.

There were other moments in the Prophet's life when it would have been understandable for even the best of people to become offended or angry, but the Prophet's *adab* was like a shining sun. The following is one of the most striking examples:

Before going to the Battle of Uhud, the Prophet had a dream which convinced him that it would be better to stay in Medina and defend it. Indeed, his dreams corresponded so closely to reality that when the Prophet had a dream, it would come about the very next day. "If the Prophet had such a dream," the people said, "it must be a revelation." Before the Battle of Uhud, he dreamed that one of his closest friends would be martyred there. He also was informed that there would be a breach in the ranks.

So the Prophet insisted at first that the Muslims should not leave Medina, but there was a group who were so eager to prove their loyalty and serve Islam that they were blinded to the subtleties of obedience; this group did not defer to his command.

After this, we can see the peerless *adab* of God's Messenger. He sat down with the company to discuss and decide together what should be done. When the group decision went against the Prophet's opinion, he did not force them. This is the *adab* of a leader. Had he insisted, the Companions certainly would have listened to him; but this carried with it the risk—even if it was one in a thousand—of creating dissention and discontent among them. Thus, the exemplar of compassion acted out of consideration for them, and let the decision stand. God's Messenger did not want any resentment to be felt in such circumstances. A little later, the Companions informed him that they had changed their minds and accepted his opinion. But he had already put on his armor and having decided to follow the majority decision, he did not remove it.

Thus, the Muslims marched toward the Battle of Uhud. Prophet Muhammad, peace and blessings be upon him, as their commander, organized them in the best possible way. The battle began and they fought hard; soon the enemy gave up and began to retreat. But here, too, some of the Muslims had not yet completely understood the subtleties of obeying as an army. The Prophet told the archers not to leave the spot where he had placed them, no matter what happened, stating, "Even if you see the eagles fly off with our flesh, do not leave your place. Even if you see us dividing the spoils, you must not leave your place...." But apparently they did not understand the gravity of his words and they must have thought he meant that they were to stay only as long as the fighting continued. When the enemy began running away they believed it was useless for them to continue waiting there, but thought that it was time to go and help their friends.

The end is well known. Sixty-nine people were slaughtered and became martyrs that day, including the Prophet's uncle, Hamza. Of those who lived, none escaped without injury. Moreover, the dignity and honor of Islam had taken a blow. For the Muslims, this was the worst of all. Now it would have been very normal for the leader of this army to become angry. But at that instant, God intervened and a verse was revealed to him:

> It was by a mercy from God that (at the time of the setback), you (O Messenger) were lenient with your followers. Had you been harsh and hard-hearted, they would surely have scattered away from about you. Then pardon them, pray for their forgiveness, and take counsel with them in the affairs (of public concern), and when you are resolved (on a course of action), put your trust in God. Surely God loves those who put their trust (in Him). (Al Imran 3:159)

The manner of address God uses here with him is revealing. For example, God does not say, "Do not be harsh and angry!" but rather, "If you had been harsh and angry" which implies that the Prophet was not. The verse continues, "*If you had been so, they would have scattered away from you,*" meaning, "Therefore treat them as your high *adab* requires and do not be severe with them."

Thus God prevented His Messenger from committing a wrong. The verse goes further than suggesting that there were no negative feelings on the part of the Prophet. God commands, "Forgive them and pray for their forgiveness!" For they needed to be released from the actions that had caused such a shadow to fall over them. For that reason the Prophet was to "ask God's forgiveness for them."

Moreover, because they had acted contrary to the Prophet's orders, they were now burdened with guilt. As long as this condition persisted they would always consider themselves to be guilty and blame themselves. Thus, the Prophet continued to call them and discuss future decisions with them as if nothing had happened, allowing them to move on.

Thus, at this most critical moment, instead of God's Messenger reacting with terrible anger, as would have been perfectly natural, God not only prevented him from expressing anger or severity. He imparted to the Prophet the most perfect *adab*.

Anas ibn Malik, who entered the Prophet's service when he was just ten years old, spoke of an experience that also demonstrated the Prophet's tolerance and gentleness: "For ten years I served God's Messenger, peace and blessings be upon him. Not once did he ever ask me, 'Why did you do this?' or 'Why didn't you do that?' In fact, one day, he sent me out with a task. On the street, I became absorbed in playing a game. I don't know how much time passed. Some time later I felt someone grasp my ear from behind. I turned around and there was the Messenger. On his face, as always, was a smile. 'I'm going right away!' I said and ran to complete my task."

God gave the Prophet strong ethics and character, and commanded him to teach the same ethics and character to his followers. To learn these ethics and this character there are two main sources we can turn to—the Qur'an and the *adab* of God's Messenger, that is, the example of Prophet Muhammad, peace and blessings be upon him.

Arranging our individual, family, and social life in conformity with the *adab* of God's Messenger means living our lives according to the Qur'an. Thus, all our questions about "how and toward whom does one act with *adab*?" will be answered.

The Companions had this *adab* of the Prophet, and therefore were extremely respectful toward him. When they listened to him, they listened with great attention, totally still and silent. They knew him and their great love for him gave rise to such respect; the more they knew him, the deeper their respect grew. There were very few of them who were comfortable enough to exchange casual words with the Prophet. The majority of the Companions would wait expectantly for times when some outsider would come and ask him something, so they could listen to his answer; they coveted such chances. This was not because he put any kind of constraints on them. Perhaps it was their response to the seriousness, dignity, and solemnity of his person. Whenever the Prophet entered a room, his followers would stand up and remain standing until he sat down because their inner respect for him moved them to do so. He would always tell them many times not to do this, and insist that they stop.

During the Treaty of Hudaybiya, an envoy observed the attitude the Companions demonstrated towards God's Messenger; the
envoy was amazed, and when he returned to Mecca he said to his
superiors, "I have been in the palaces of Khosrau, I have stayed as
a guest in the palaces of Byzantine kings, and I have seen many
great rulers and sovereigns. Some of them were tyrants and des-
pots. But I have never in my life seen anyone treat their leader
with so much sincere respect as Muhammad's followers."

Amr ibn As was one of the best-known politicians of the time.
Right before he died, he took something out of his pocket and
said, "Place this under my tongue." They asked him what it was.
He answered, "A hair from the head of God's Messenger." He had
such profound love and respect for the Prophet, and he believed it
would give him comfort when he is called to account before God.

Abu Bakr once had an argument with a Jewish man. Each one
of them claimed that their Prophet was greater. At length the
Jewish man said something unkind about Prophet Muhammad,
peace and blessings be upon him, and so Abu Bakr, who loved the
Prophet, slapped him. The Jewish man went immediately to the
Prophet and told him about this. The Prophet declared, "Do not
hold me in greater esteem than Moses."

Another time, when the verse, *"(O Muhammad) Do not be like
the companion of the fish,"* (Qalam 68:48) was revealed, the Prophet
clarified it, so that no one would get wrong ideas about this Prophet,
"Do not distinguish between me and Prophet Jonah," thus not allowing his followers to consider him greater than Prophet Jonah.

Indeed, God's Messenger was given that which no other
Prophet had been given. Every Prophet communicated either directly or indirectly with God; however, none was granted the
Ascension (*Miraj*) except God's Messenger. As all the hosts looked
on in wonder, he was taken through the heavenly dimensions of
existence and was shown both Heaven and Hell. What an honor
to be in the community of followers of God's Messenger, for the
Almighty granted him a blessing during the Ascension, and he

brought this amazing gift to us—the five daily Prayers, or the ascension of the believers. God blessed us with this in the most perfect way through our Prophet.

Following the example of the Best of Creation, it is absolutely essential that we claim this inheritance, bringing the light of his *adab* to our lives. It is incumbent upon Muslims that his practices be followed in obligatory acts of worship, as he was the most perfect practitioner; it is also encouraged that we follow his example in all matters.

The Prophet always actively helped his friends with any task that needed to be done. At home he helped his wives. He never asked others to do his personal chores for him. Naturally, there were many people who would have gladly done anything for him. But when there was a task to be done he was always the first to start working. For example, one day the Prophet was on a journey and dinnertime came. One of the Companions said, "I'll slaughter a sheep." Another said, "I'll skin it." The Prophet said immediately, "I'll gather the firewood," and went to get it. For the Battle of the Trench he dug trenches alongside everyone else, and when the community built a mosque he carried the bricks with everyone else. Because he acted in this way, his friends also began to act thus.

What we know of the Prophet's lifestyle, including how he dressed, ate, drank and slept, has been passed down to us as part of our heritage. His ways of living were completely natural and in accordance with human nature. The Prophet's way of life was not merely an ideal, it is something that can be easily realized. This means that there is an example of perfect *adab* in the Messenger of God for the people of today and tomorrow. This is the *adab* that can lead both individuals and communities to salvation.

M. Fethullah Gülen

PREFACE

I n the name of God, the All-Merciful, the All-Compassionate: All praise and thanks be to God, the Creator and Sustainer of all the worlds, and endless peace and blessings be on His Messenger. This work is intended as an explanation of various aspects of *adab*, or manners, one of the most essential elements of human life.

There are a few individual works regarding this topic already in existence. In addition, a few other, basic articles within larger works may be found. However, there exists a need for further separate works completely devoted to this topic. I have attempted, in creating this work, to fulfill that need to some small degree.

As is known, the roots of morality and ethics are to be found in the two hallowed sources of Islam, the Qur'an and the practices of Prophet Muhammad, peace and blessings be upon him. It would not be an overstatement to say that there is no foundational principle of ethics that cannot be found in Islam. The Revelation is a constant bounty of our Lord that is given to us from His Infinite Mercy; it is He, our Creator, Who knows human nature best of all. For these reasons, I begin each section with Qur'anic verses and try to further clarify each issue with the practices of Prophet Muhammad, peace and blessings be upon him. As a third source of information, I have referred to the scholarly opinions of the most respected Islamic scholars on the issues.

There is an effort to enable practical application for the benefit of the reader by addressing topics one at a time.

The author would be grateful if the readers would indicate any mistakes or omissions in the text. It is hoped that this book will be beneficial and useful for all.

Musa Kazım Gülçür
Istanbul, 2008

CHAPTER 1

Character and Ethics

BUILDING GOOD CHARACTER

The topic of this book, "*adab* in practice," is part of the larger concept of *akhlaq*, that is, morality. In fact, from one perspective, *adab* in practice is fundamentally practical morality and ethics. Therefore, the essence of these concepts will be explained first, beginning with a short introduction to *akhlaq*, and only after this will *adab* in practice be returned to.

Akhlaq, the plural of *khuluq* in Arabic, means the character and temperament of a person. The temperament of a person brings either good or harmful things. In the broadest aspect morality means that there is a moral character, that is, morality becomes deeply ingrained in the soul and as a consequence right actions and behavior come naturally and easily from within; then, the person with such a character no longer has to struggle intellectually to know what ethical choices to make.

Human characteristics can generally be divided into those that society approves of and those that we disapprove of. Decency, humility, and kindness are traits that are seen in a positive light, while arrogance, deceit, and miserliness are generally perceived as negative human characteristics. To recognize these characteristics and their attendant traits is to understand what is meant here by the phrase "moral character." Nawwas ibn Saman once asked the Prophet how to recognize the difference between goodness and sin. The Prophet answered, "Goodness is good moral character. Sin is anything that pricks one's conscience, and which one does not want others to know about."[1] Another narration from Jabir reports that the Messenger said, "The most beloved to me among you and the ones who will be closest to me on the Day of Judgment are the best in moral character. And they who are most loathsome to me and will be farthest from me on the Day of Judgment are those who gossip, those with unbridled tongues, and those who condescend." When they asked him, "O Messenger of God! Who are those who condescend?" he replied, "They are those who are arrogant."[2]

Ethics, which is the study or science of morals, can be divided into the theoretical and the practical. While theoretical morality is concerned with those concepts that constitute the principles and rules of morality, practical morality is concerned with the duties that constitute the basis of a moral life. As reported by the Prophet, "God looks not at your outward appearances, nor at your wealth or belongings. God looks only at your hearts and your deeds."[3] For this reason, here we will be mainly concerned with the practical side of morality, and as mentioned above, the purpose of this book is to explore *adab* in practice. At this point, with a view to clarifying the meaning of human responsibility, let us take a closer look at the concept of duty, which is pivotal to developing a good character with *adab*.

THE NATURE AND TYPES OF DUTY

Duty is the moral responsibility of a person who has reached puberty when they have been asked to do something good or helpful. Accordingly, Islamically there are two types of duty. One is the obligatory (*fard*) group of duties, that is, those the performance of which is binding and the abandonment of which is forbidden. For example, performing daily prayers, fasting during the holy month of Ramadan, and offering prescribed purifying alms fall into this category. The other type of duty is that which, although not obligatory, is encouraged or desirable; it is these duties that religion presents as being inherent parts of a good moral character. To observe these duties on top of the obligatory ones shows greater spiritual maturity and is worthy of Divine reward; the observation of them pleases God. To neglect such duties would be a shortcoming. An example of this type of duty would be the giving of money or goods to those in need (*sadaqa*), over and above the prescribed purifying alms (*zakat*), and generally being kind and polite to everyone.

Duties can further be classified as those fulfilled in the cause of God, or for the benefit of the individual, family, or even society. From this perspective, duties can be divided into different sorts—divine, familial, and social duties. Let us more closely examine these categories.

Divinely-Ordained Duties

It is incumbent upon every person who has come of age and who is in possession of all their mental faculties that they recognize and worship God. For a human there can be no greater blessing or honor than this servitude to God. One worships God by willingly and gratefully performing acts of worship, such as daily prayers, fasting, charity, and such other commitments that require both physical and financial abilities, like the pilgrimage to Mecca. In addition to these duties that pertain to the personal practice of Islam, safeguarding and defending one's homeland is also a sacred duty.

Another very important divine duty is to struggle against one's own evil-commanding soul. Those who cannot discipline their ego or self through moral education will not be able to help themselves, let alone society. Believers, both as individuals and members of society, need to exert themselves to strive in the way of God in all their actions at all moments of life. This is what Prophet Muhammad, peace and blessings be upon him, meant when he said, "We are returning from the lesser *jihad* (struggle) to the greater," while he was returning to Medina from the Campaign of Tabuk.[4] Emphasizing that they were returning from "the lesser struggle to the greater," the Prophet directed his Community to this "greater struggle" that is waged against one's carnal self at all moments of life.

Being this comprehensive in nature, *jihad* includes every action, from the simplest act of speaking to remaining silent or performing supererogatory acts of worship, such as extra prayers, worship and fasting to attain the good pleasure of God. Likewise, to enlighten our hearts we can read the Qur'an, or to increase the light of our faith we can continually remember and reflect on the Divine Attributes of our Almighty Creator that are manifest all around us.

Individual Duties

Each person has some duties toward their own self as well. Some of these pertain to the body, and some to the spirit. The following are the main duties that fall into this category:

1. Training the body: For everyone it is crucial that the body be kept strong and clean. Prophet Muhammad, peace and blessings be upon him, said, "A strong and vigorous believer is better than a frail and weak one."[5]

2. Caring for one's health: Health is a great blessing; therefore, it is vital to avoid things that may damage one's health and to seek treatment when one is ill.

3. Refraining from dangerous practices of abstinence or self-denial practiced in the name of spiritual discipline.

4. Guarding against things that wear down and age the body.

5. Strengthening willpower: A person needs to develop healthy self-control. This involves learning what is good for the body and partaking of it, as well as finding out what is harmful and avoiding it.

6. Duties relating to the mind and intellect, such as pursuing learning and enlightenment, awakening higher emotions and positive feelings in the heart, and honing one's talents and skills.

Family Duties

The family is the very foundation of a healthy society. Each member of the family must accept some responsibility for the others in the family. Some of the primary duties of a husband, for instance, are to behave kindly toward his wife, to meet her basic needs, and to be loyal to her. A narration of the Prophet says, "The best of you is he who is the best to his wife."[6] A wife who is happy with her spouse will support her husband's decisions, as long as they do not conflict with religious directives and contribute to protecting the family honor and property. All these are pivotal to happiness in marital relations and to a happy family.

Parents in such an atmosphere commit themselves to nurturing, educating and training their children to the best of their ability, setting them on the path to success in life. Fathers and mothers should treat their children equally, holding them in equal regard and affection. They should be gentle towards their offspring, and raise them in such a way that they will not be inclined to rebel. Parents also have the duty to be models of virtue for their children.

Respect and obedience are, in turn, some of the basic duties of children towards parents who have brought them up according to the principles set out above and with love and compassion, feeding and caring for them. This is why children should not show displeasure or impatience with their parents. A son or daughter who ignores the wishes of their parents and does not heed them nor come to their assistance if they are in need is not a source of blessing for the parents. Such a person not only is not a useful member of society, but will also stand before God as one who is guilty of shirking their duty.

Likewise, siblings have duties toward one another, such as showing affection and compassion for each other, as well as helping and respecting each other. There is a very strong bond between brothers and sisters and this should be maintained at all times. Brothers and sisters who cut their ties with one another over finances or property disagreements cannot be considered to be blessed or benevolent. Finally, if a household has hired help, this helper also must be treated as part of the family. They deserve kindness and gentle treatment and should never be overloaded with work that is too difficult for them to carry out.

Social Duties

Human beings have been created as social beings, and as such they live in social groups and have formed civilizations. Socializing is one of our basic needs, and social life involves certain expectations between people. When these are disregarded, society breaks down and people can no longer coexist peacefully or work together. The main responsibilities in this category are the preservation of the following inalienable rights:

1. Protecting the life of every individual: Every person has the right to life. No one has the right to take another person's life. According to Islam, one who wrongfully kills a person is as guilty as if they have murdered all of humanity; likewise, one who saves one person's life is as blessed as if they have saved all of humanity.

2. Safeguarding the freedom of all people: God Almighty created every human being free and equal. At the same time, it is certain that this freedom has boundaries. We do not have the prerogative to do anything we want; if we had such freedom this would violate the freedoms of others.

3. The consideration of conscience: When a person has a well-functioning conscience, this allows them to differentiate between good and bad. The value of such a conscience can be better understood if one observes outward consequences. A person who engages in incorrect behavior cannot be said to have a functioning conscience. Islam assigns great importance to having a conscience that helps one to be concerned for the happiness and guidance of all humanity.

To this end, it encourages pity towards those who have a faulty conscience, and tries to bring them to the right way. One can never try to control or rule another person's conscience; this is the province of God alone. Each person will be rewarded or punished for what is in their conscience. However, this does not mean it is wrong to admonish or advise a person who has a bad conscience, if the idea is to help the person.

4. Protecting freedom of mind: Any thought or opinion, right or wrong, must be approached in a scholarly manner. This is the only way for a truth to be discovered, and it is also the only way for society to prove the harmfulness of false ideas.

5. Protecting the honor and reputation of individuals: In Islam, everyone has the right to maintain their honor and dignity. Any attack against honor or dignity, we have been taught, will be gravely punished. It is for this reason that gossip, slander, ridicule, the cursing of others and saying negative things about others are absolutely forbidden in Islam.

6. The preservation of other people's property: It is also forbidden to usurp the property or possessions of any other person. What is earned by a person belongs strictly to that person. This is essential for the development of a civilized society. It is reasonable and necessary that the individuals who make up a society will have different degrees of wealth, according to their profession and training. In a fair and equitable society all should be grateful for and satisfied with their own portion.

THE ETHICS OF DECENT
BEHAVIOR IN ISLAM

B efore examining the ethics of decent behavior (*adab al-muasharat*) in depth, the concepts of *adab* and *muasharat* first should be examined separately.

THE WORD *ADAB*

The Arabic root *"adb"* means "feast or invitation"[7]; the word *"ad-ab,"* which is derived from this root, carries the meanings of "decency," "politeness," "reverence," and "high regard,"[8] as well as "refined manners that have been socially adopted."[9]

Adab, then, refers to all guidelines about words and deeds that are considered proper, mannerly, ethical, and morally correct in Islam. In this respect, *adab* indicates the minimum level of good or moral behavior that people should follow. In his book *Al-Tarifat* Sayyid Sharif writes that *adab* "is the knowledge that saves one from erring." Ibn Hajar said that *"Adab* is to say and do that which is commendable and of merit; that is, to possess good moral character. In the same way that there are people who interpret *adab* as meaning 'acting in good and appropriate ways,' or 'acting respectfully towards elders and treating the young with kindness and compassion' there are also scholars who believe the word originated from *madaba,* a word that means *banquet.*"[10]

There is no direct reference to the word *adab* or its derivatives in the Qur'an. However, the related word *da'b*, which means *way, path, manner,* or *custom,* is used, for instance in the verse, *"(Their way is) as the way of Pharaoh's folk and those before them"* (Anfal 8:54). Similarly, *daab,* which appears in the verse, *"You shall sow for seven years as usual,*" (Yusuf 12:47) means *as usual*. In yet another verse, the related word *daibayn* is used to mean *constant*: "*And He has made the sun and the moon constant in their courses...*" (Ibrahim 14:33). However, the word *adab* does appear in Prophetic traditions. In the hadith, "My Lord trained me and gave me *adab* and He gave me the best training,"[11] *adab* is used to mean training or education.

When Junayd al-Baghdadi set out on his pilgrimage, he saw that the disciples of Abu Hafs in Baghdad were extremely mannerly and polite. He said to the scholar, "You have taught your followers *adab* that is befitting of courtiers." Abu Hafs replied, "No, their inner *adab* is reflected in their outward actions," implying that their behavior arose from their heart.[12] This is striking, as it underlines the importance of maintaining good social relationships with everyone. In fact, some have said that *adab* is an outward sign that reveals the greatness of a person's character. It is for this reason that one of the most important responsibilities of parents is to give their children *adab* and moral training. *Adab* is like a garment for the soul, or the inner strength of the spirit that saves one from erring or doing inappropriate things.

The term *adab* in Islamic jurisprudence refers to "behavior befitting the example of Prophet Muhammad, peace and blessings be upon him." Accordingly, the term *adab* implies "avoidance of anything that is contrary to the *Sunna* or the practice of the Prophet." In a broader sense, *adab* is to act in accordance with the commands and admonitions of God and His Messenger. Religiously, *adab* falls into the category of *sunna ghayr mu'akkada*, that is, actions which the Prophet performed at times; therefore, the execution of such actions is to be rewarded, but the abandonment of them is not reproachable. *Adab* is also used interchangeably for recommended (*mustahab*) acts, supererogatory acts, or virtuous acts. Acts that are defined as part of *adab* are divinely rewarded, praiseworthy manners that were recommended and encouraged by the Prophet.

The best *adab,* the best morals, those which will never become outdated, are those taught in the Qur'an and applied in the life of Prophet Muhammad, the Best of Creation. God, Who created the universe in the most perfect order and the human *"of the best stature as the perfect pattern of creation"* (Tin 95:4), has created humankind to act as His vicegerents on earth. He has given humankind superiority over all other creatures and made them His representatives on earth. Through His Messengers God has shown humankind the path to felicity, and, by making His commandments known to us, He has taught us to discern good from bad and right from wrong. God has created all things perfectly, and has instructed humanity in the ways of goodness that we should follow. This is why the *adab* and morality which God taught us will always be the best and most correct. The person who has lived these morals the best is Prophet Muhammad, peace and blessings be upon him. In a Qur'anic verse God says of the Prophet, *"You are surely of a sublime character and do act by a sublime pattern of conduct"* (68:4). God's Messenger said of himself "I was sent to perfect good character."[13] He exhorted his community to apply the morality and ethics in the Qur'an which he put into practice.

As with everything, our example in good morals is Prophet Muhammad, the Best of Creation: *"Assuredly you have in God's Messenger an excellent example to follow for whoever looks forward to God and the Last Day, and remembers and mentions God much"* (Ahzab 33:21). God's Messenger called on us to pursue morality, and he said, "Two qualities are never coupled in a believer: Stinginess and corrupt morality."[14] Another time, he said to Muadh ibn Jabal, "O Muadh, be of good morals toward people!"[15]

The Messenger of God taught that good morality will weigh heaviest in the scales for a believer on the Day of Judgment; those with an evil disposition will be condemned. He also told another Companion that people with good morality would be dealt with (rewarded) as if they had worshipped and fasted constantly.[16]

When Prophet Muhammad, peace and blessings be upon him, was performing *salat*, after saying the opening *takbir* he would sometimes recite the prayer that has the following meaning: "My prayer, my worship, my living and my dying are for God, the Lord of the worlds. No associate has He, I have thus been commanded. And I am the first and foremost of those who submit to Him. O God, guide me to the best deeds and the best morality. There is none other than You who can lead me to the best. Save me from evil deeds and conduct; there is none other than You who can save us from immorality."[17]

When the Prophet was asked what it was that caused most people to be sent to Hell, he replied, "The mouth and the genitals." When they asked him what brought most people to Heaven, he said, "*Taqwa* (God-consciousness and fear of God) and good morals!"[18]

Here it may be helpful to go into detail about the term *taqwa*. Generally, this word is used in one of two ways:

The first broad meaning is "to beware of and avoid everything which is harmful for the eternal life of one's soul," or, more importantly, "to eschew associating partners to God, which is the cause of spending eternity in Hell." The highest point of *taqwa* is to keep oneself pure of anything that could put a distance between one's soul and God, to turn to God with one's entire being, and to take refuge in God with one's whole spirit. A Qur'anic verse indicates this state: "*O you who have attained faith! Be conscious of God with all the consciousness that is due to Him...*" (Al Imran 3:102).

The second specific meaning is absolutely and unequivocally "to guard oneself against any sin which may be cause for the abandonment of good deeds or which may lead one away from salvation." The verse, "*Those who avoid the major sins and indecent, shameful deeds, only falling into small fault,—surely your Lord is of extensive forgiveness*" (Najm 53:32), focuses on this meaning of *taqwa*—that is the avoidance of major sins.

Raghib al-Isfahani says, "*Taqwa* is to keep one's soul from sin; this is begun by avoiding that which is forbidden, and completed by avoiding that which is questionable. According to the hadith, 'The permissible is clear, and the forbidden is clear, but there are questionable things in between.'"[19]

Here we must briefly touch upon the subject of "small sins." The aforementioned verse of Sura Najm does not mean that believers can be lax about "small sins." Said ibn Jubayr reportedly said, "When the following Qur'anic verse was revealed: '*They give to the poor, orphans and slaves solely for God's pleasure, even when they themselves are in need*' (Insan 76:8), some Muslims thought that because they had given only a little they would not be rewarded; others thought, 'God will reserve Hellfire for great sins,' and they did not think that they would be punished for smaller sins, like lying, looking at forbidden things, or gossiping. For this reason, God sent down another verse, '*And so, he who shall have done an atom's weight of good, shall behold it; and he who shall have done an atom's weight of evil, shall behold it*' (Zilzal 99:7–8). Through these verses God taught Muslims that 'A little will soon bring more,' thus encouraging them to give without thinking that small offerings do not count; on the other hand, they were given the idea that 'small sins soon increase and lead to greater sins,' thus helping them to avoid all sins."[20]

According to Islamic teachings, a small sin can be as serious as a large one if the following errors occur:

1. Persistence in small sins.
2. Considering small sins lightly, attaching no importance to them.
3. Making oneself feel better about small sins by comparing them to bigger ones.
4. Boasting of one's past sins in front of other people.
5. The commitment of small sins by a knowledgeable person who is acting as a guide for others; these must be counted as serious sins.

What should be kept in mind is that whatever God has forbidden should not be approached, refuge from both small and great sins should be sought in God, whatever is given as a sin in the Qur'an should be accepted as a sin, and if one commits a sin, it should not be persisted in. Indeed, Prophet Muhammad, peace and blessings be upon him, said, "When we repent and regret a 'great sin,' it is no longer 'great,' but when we persist in a 'small sin' it does not remain 'small.'"[21]

To return to our main topic, let us examine the following hadith of the Prophet: "A believer who has good morals may surpass one who spends nights in prayer and days in fasting."[22] He also informed Abu Hurayra, in response to a question, that one may enter Heaven with fear of God and the possession of good morals. More than once the Prophet said that a person of good morals will be rewarded with a home in the upper levels of Heaven; such a person will be the closest to the Prophets on the Day of Resurrection and he will be the most loved by them.[23]

The sayings and personal actions of the Prophet regarding his guidelines for good *adab* and morals have been classified and collected into books like *The Book of Adab* and *Bab al-Adab*.[24] In addition, Imam al-Bukhari compiled some deeds and sayings of the Prophet in his book *Al-Adab al-Mufrad*.

Adab means acting with good manners, ethics and morals in all interactions and dealings with people. The behavior that we find in the life of Prophet Muhammad, peace and blessings be upon him, even actions in minor matters, like greeting people, smiling, and keeping nails trimmed, were also part of the lives of other Prophets before him.

The *adab* and moral code established by the hadiths of the Prophet are applicable to everyone. Therefore, every person who is involved in teaching or training others in *adab* must first put into practice these commands and prohibitions, then strive to impart the same good ethics to those under their care. God says in the Qur'an, "*O you who believe! Guard yourselves and your families (through the enabling discipline of Islamic faith and worship) against a Fire whose fuel is human beings and stones...*" (Talaq 66:6). Here it is meant that God wants us to practice the morality He has prescribed, both by training our spirits and by training the children for whom we have a responsibility. This will at the same time be a protection for us from the fire of Hell.

Everyone has responsibility for those under their care and supervision with regard to their rights, education, and learning. God's Messenger spoke of the importance of the education of children by their parents thus: "Every child is born in the natural state of innate predisposition for goodness and submission to One God. Afterward, the mother and father teach a child another religion. Indeed, even animal young are born complete (with all they need for life). Have you ever seen among these innocent newborn animals one with a cut-off arm, lip, leg, foot, nose?"[25] Abu Hurayra, the transmitter of this hadith, then continued with this verse: "*And so, set your face steadfastly toward the (one ever-true) faith, turning away from all that is false, in accordance with the natural disposition which God has instilled into man...*" (Rum 30:30).

The verse and hadith above point to the fact that the natural state of the human being is pure and that the best and purest morality one can follow is Islam. But incorrect education can make a child become alienated from their inborn natural purity and grow into a disbeliever or someone with bad morals. This is why the environment and parental influence on children is emphasized so strongly.[26] God creates each individual with purity, and the mother and father of each child have the duty to bring out and preserve that nature by teaching *adab*. The best and most lasting gift parents can give their children is a good moral training. A child who receives this training and grows to be a good person will also become a source of continual reward for the parents; even after they are dead and can no longer perform good deeds, the child's good deeds will be reflected on them and be recorded in their Book of Deeds by God.

THE WORD *MUASHARAT* (SOCIAL ETIQUETTE)

The word *muasharat* has several meanings: to mix or become involved, to be a friend, to live together.[27] The religion of Islam puts great importance on positive social relations between human beings—spending time together and talking to one another—and their shared community. After this brief introduction to the *adab al-muasharat* (ethics of decent behavior in Islam) we will examine good character traits in the light of Qur'anic verses and hadith.

CHAPTER 2

Good Education and Upbringing

STUDYING AND LEARNING

The basis of acquiring knowledge is reading and studying. The first revelation of God's Word to Muhammad (peace and blessings be upon him), the first command of his Prophethood, began with the command, "Read!" This announced a fundamental principle. Let us revisit these verses in Sura Alaq, the first verses of the Qur'an to be revealed:

> (1) Read in and with the Name of your Lord, Who has created–
> (2) created man from a clot clinging (to the wall of the womb)!
> (3) Read, and your Lord is the All-Munificent,
> (4) Who has taught (man) by the pen–
> (5) taught man what he did not know! (96:1–5)

The first revelation begins with the command to read the miracle of creation through faith in God and knowledge of Him. Then it refers to the creation of human beings, encouraging contemplation on this miraculous occurrence in the second verse. It continues with another directive to "read," and refers to "the pen," "teaching/learning" (between God and people), "knowing" and "knowledge." It is one of God's great blessings that man, at first an insignificant being, was given knowledge that elevated humankind to the highest level over all other creatures. Being taught not only knowledge, but also the use of the pen, humankind has thus been entrusted with the duty of spreading this knowledge far and wide, using it for development and progress, and preserving it for future generations. If it were not for the revelation of God and the blessings of abilities that are represented by "the pen" and "the book," humanity could not have accomplished all the achievements that have been constructed on the accumulated wisdom of centuries.

The basic state of humanity was unenlightened until God blessed us, allowing us to grow in knowledge. At every stage knowledge was given as a blessing and the doors of learning were opened by God. That which people thought they themselves had developed, in truth was given to them by their Creator without their realizing it. For this reason, everyone who has some knowledge should recognize the true Source of such blessings, praising and turning to the One Who granted them, and employing them in a manner that is pleasing to God. This will ensure that knowledge will never separate a person from God or cause them to forget Him.

Any "knowledge" that distances a person from their Creator is divorced from its basic purpose. It can never be of benefit to people or make them happy, for it can produce only evil, depression, or destruction. As such knowledge has deviated from the Source of knowledge it has lost its direction and no longer leads to the Path of God. Therefore, it is crucial that someone who attains knowledge not forget, even for a moment, that the power and authority the knowledge has brought can be used for right or for wrong, and all persons will be responsible to the Originator of that knowledge for the way it is used.

"Knowledge is power," or as the Qur'an says, "*...whoever is granted the Wisdom has indeed been granted much good*" (Baqara 2:269). In this verse, the word *al-hikma*—often translated as "the Wisdom"—means "beneficial knowledge." Knowledge that is beneficial to people will also elevate the status of the person who knows. The Qur'an also says that those who *know* God cannot be on the same level with those who do not: "*Is he who worships God devoutly in the watches of the night prostrating and standing, who fears the Hereafter and hopes for the mercy of his Lord (to be likened to that other)? Say: 'Are they ever equal, those who know and those who do not know?' Only the people of discernment will reflect on (the distinction between knowledge and ignorance, and obedience to God and disobedience,) and be mindful*" (Zumar 39:9). This last verse makes it clear that knowledge must be used together with the ability to reason, drawing particular attention to the fact that any knowledge based on knowledge of God is true knowledge and beneficial to those who possess it. In fact, knowledge has a potentially destructive power in the hands of those who do not use their reason, merely acting in sheer ignorance of God. Beyond this basic *adab* of knowledge, let us now examine the further sayings of Prophet Muhammad, peace and blessings be upon him, on this topic.

At every opportunity, the Prophet drew attention to the importance of knowledge. One day he said to Abu Dharr, "O Abu Dharr, if you leave your home in the morning to go out to learn a verse of the Qur'an, this holds more blessings for you than performing a hundred *rakats* of supererogatory prayer. And if you leave your home in the morning to go out to acquire knowledge, this holds more benefit for you than performing a thousand *rakats* of supererogatory prayer."[1] In another hadith God's Messenger said, "When God wills blessings for someone, He makes them knowledgeable in religion."[2]

Moreover, keeping knowledge from people, unless one is forced to by circumstances, is not a desirable act. This was made clear by the Prophet, who said, "If someone is asked to share their knowledge but they hide it and do not speak, they will be bridled with a bridle of fire (on the Judgment Day)."[3]

The Prophet also made it known that spiritual knowledge, which puts a person on the right path and leads to righteousness, is more valuable than the greatest worldly treasures: "By God, it is better for you that God should give guidance to a single person on the right path through you than that you should acquire a whole herd of red camels."[4] At this time, red camels were very precious, and a person who owned such a camel was rich; extremely few people owned an entire herd of red camels. This comparison, therefore, clearly shows the value of knowledge that leads to good, and of leading others to good.

Yazid ibn Balama once asked, "O Messenger of God! I have memorized many of your sayings. But I am afraid that those I memorize later will make me forget those I memorized earlier. Tell me a word that will help me retain all the things I have learned without forgetting the others!" The Prophet replied, "Stay upright before God in what you have learned (and that is enough for you)!"[5]

One of the most esteemed Companions of the Prophet, Ibn Abbas, gave the following advice: "Tell people one hadith per week. If this does not seem enough, recount two or three. And never cause people to become bored with the Qur'an! When people are talking amongst themselves, never let me see you walk up and interrupt them to teach them something. When they are speaking, be quiet and listen. If they come to you and ask you to talk, then you should teach them on their request."[6]

In addition to choosing the appropriate time, it is also important when teaching ethical principles or religious knowledge to choose a level that can be understood by one's audience. Some people try to appear knowledgeable by using a style and manner which is not clear or understandable. This is wrong, as it goes against the proper manners of speaking to people in a way that makes sense to them. No less a person than Ali ibn Abu Talib said, "Tell people things they can understand. Do you want to be responsible for making God and His Messenger misunderstood?"[7] He meant that plain and clear speech should be used, especially when speaking of spiritual matters. Ibn Mas'ud also said, "If you say something to a gathering which is above their intellectual capacity, it will certainly lead some of them into mischief."[8]

Someone who lives an exemplary life and tries to please God by teaching other people and sharing knowledge is on the Path of God, and God is indeed pleased by such a person. Kathir ibn Qays explains, "I was in the Mosque at Damascus sitting beside Abu al-Darda. A man came and said, 'O Abu al-Darda, I came from the Prophet's city of Medina to ask about a hadith that I have heard you are relating.' Abu al-Darda, in order to find out whether this was really the man's intention, asked, 'Could you also have come to do business (trade)?' 'No,' he answered, 'I did not come to do any such thing.' He asked again, 'So you did not come for anything else other than to hear a hadith?' The man replied, 'No, I came only because I heard that you know hadith.' Only when he had established that the man had truly come to win God's pleasure did Abu al-Darda say, 'I heard the Prophet of God say, "God will make the path to Heaven easy to anyone who takes to the road looking for knowledge. Angels lower their wings over the seeker of knowledge, being pleased with what he does. All the creatures in the earth and sky, even the fish in the sea, pray for God's help and forgiveness for those who acquire knowledge. The superiority of the scholar over the worshipper is like the superiority of the moon over the stars (i.e., in brightness). Scholars are the heirs to the Prophets. For the Prophets left neither *dinar* nor *dirham* (units of money) but knowledge as their inheritance. Therefore he who acquires knowledge has in fact acquired an abundant portion.""""[9]

The following points can be deduced from the hadith:

1. Any effort or endeavor that is expended on acquiring knowledge is counted as effort or struggle made on God's way, and this leads a person to Paradise. To put it simply, the path of knowledge is the path to Heaven; what a beautiful path it is. The angels come to the aid of one who is on this path, and all creation offers prayers for them.

2. The difference between the scholar and the follower is like the difference between the moon and stars, for knowledge is a light that illuminates a person's whole surroundings and the community of the knowledgeable person. It shows the right path to everyone. However, a person who simply follows, even if they perform a great deal of supererogatory worship, does not benefit others in the same way. Their worship benefits only themselves. Those who

choose knowledge, on the other hand, bring blessings down upon themselves and all those around them.

3. Scholars are the heirs to the Prophets; the only thing the Prophets left as an inheritance was knowledge. When scholars choose the path of learning and the pursuit of knowledge, they win the honor of inheriting the legacy of the Prophets. One of the Prophet's Companions, Abu Hurayra, was almost always at the Prophet's side. He would listen to all the Prophet's teachings, carefully memorizing his sayings. One day in Medina, he spoke aloud to the people milling about on the street: "The Prophet's inheritance is being divided up; why are you wasting time here? Go and claim your share!" The people said, "Where is it being distributed?" Abu Hurayra said, "In the mosque." So they ran to the mosque. But soon they turned around and came back, and Abu Hurayra asked, "What's happened?" They said, "We went to the mosque, but we did not see anything like what you said being distributed." So he asked, "Was there no one in the mosque?" They answered, "Yes, we saw some people; some of them were praying *salat*, some were reading the Qur'an, and some were talking about the permissible and the prohibited." Hearing this, Abu Hurayra told them, "Shame on you. That was the Prophet's inheritance."[10]

The Qur'an mentions the *adab* of sitting in the gatherings where a scholar or spiritual guide is teaching to increase one's faith and knowledge:

> O you who believe! When you are told, "Make room in the assemblies (for one another and for new comers)," do make room. God will make room for you (in His grace and Paradise). And when you are told, "Rise up (and leave the assembly)," then do rise up. God will raise (in degree) those of you who truly believe (and act accordingly), and in degrees those who have been granted the knowledge (especially of reli-

gious matters). Surely God is fully aware of all that you do. (Mujadila 58:11)

When knowledge, which leads one to greater piety and a better religious life, and allows others to benefit, is added to faith, God will exalt its owner by many ranks. God commanded the Prophet, *"(O Muhammad,) Say, 'O my Lord, increase me in knowledge!'"* (TaHa 20:114).

In full submission to this Divine order, the Prophet prayed, "O God, make the knowledge You have taught me benefit me, and continue to teach me knowledge that will benefit me. Increase me in knowledge. God be praised at all times."[11] This prayer in which Prophet Muhammad, peace and blessings be upon him, asks God to make his knowledge beneficial to him is also complemented by another prayer in which he sought refuge in God from knowledge that would not prove beneficial.

Why do humans learn? Why should knowledgeable people be so highly regarded above all others? The answer to these questions can be found in the Qur'an: *"Of all His servants, only those possessed of true knowledge stand in awe of God..."* (Fatir 35:28). So it can be said that one reason for this is that scholars make it possible for others to know God better and to better understand the message of the Prophets of God.

God's Messenger taught that it was worthwhile to envy two things. One of these is when someone takes the possessions God has bestowed on them and spends them in the way of God. The other is when someone blessed with knowledge and wisdom becomes a teacher and shares that wisdom with others.[12] This means that when one acquires knowledge, one should then teach it to others; it is not wrong to "envy" (desire to be like) a person who does this.

The Prophet said the following regarding studying, literacy, education, making our knowledge a source of good for others, and educating others: "It is incumbent upon all Muslims to acquire knowledge."[13] As we can see, studying and learning are of critical importance in Islam. These hadith confirm the Prophet's teaching,

"Knowledge and wisdom are the common property of every believer; wherever they are found, they should be acquired."[14]

The technology we have today is without a doubt the product of knowledge. It is easy to understand, looking from the perspective of the heights of knowledge, from the science and technology that have been achieved in the modern world, why Islam emphasizes knowledge and education so strongly. Is it possible to ignore its importance when we are surrounded by all the useful fruits and products of intellectual inquiry? Certainly we must listen well to the teachings of Islam on this matter and show greater concern for educating the next generation if we are to solve some of the current harmful trends. Instead of leaving them material possessions, we should spend our money to make sure they receive opportunities to become truly "rich" in knowledge. Ali ibn Abu Talib said, "Someone who has money will have to protect it, whereas a person who has knowledge will be protected by it. Knowledge is a king; possessions are captives. And when possessions are spent they diminish, while knowledge increases when shared."[15] Highlighting the excellence of knowledge Prophet Muhammad, peace and blessings be upon him, said, "Be of those who teach or those who learn, those who listen, or those who love knowledge. If you are not in at least one of these groups, you are headed for destruction."[16]

The *adab* of learning applies not only to those who are teaching and learning religious studies but all types of useful knowledge. Here we give some details for our younger brothers and sisters who are students, regarding the *adab* of learning to add to what has been quoted above:

1. If at first you don't succeed do not lose heart.
2. Classes should be entered with a mind that is prepared and willing.
3. Listen to a teacher with your spiritual ears.
4. When you don't understand something, always ask.
5. Try to make friends with successful students and get tips from them.

6. Always plan and organize your time.
7. Always try to be the best.
8. Don't go on to something else until you have understood what you are working on.
9. If what you are studying is practically applicable, learn it through application.
10. Do not maintain ties with people who discourage you from learning or dislike your studying.
11. Be respectful and humble towards your teachers.

TEACHER–STUDENT RELATIONS

Ali ibn Abu Talib said, "I would be the slave of anyone who teaches me one letter." This saying expresses the great respect that is due to teachers. Throughout Islamic history, educational institutions have always remained free of association with governmental or political institutions, avoiding partiality in political debates, and thereby protecting the dignity of knowledge, even when scholars were threatened with the worst kind of persecution. Teachers did not discriminate between students according to race, class, or socioeconomic background, and tried their best to help all develop into good citizens. The Ottoman rulers did not deviate from this tradition and maintained respect for teachers. There is a famous story about Sultan Selim I, the ninth Ottoman sultan, and his teacher Ibn Kemal. When they were returning from victory at the Battle of Mercidabik in 1516 the teacher was traveling in front of the Sultan, and his horse splashed mud on the Sultan's robes. The Sultan smiled and, saying that the mud was an ornament to his robes, ordered that they be saved—unwashed—and used to cover his coffin.

PROPER ATTITUDE TOWARDS SCHOLARS

Traditionally, out of respect, we avoid calling our parents by their first names; this kind of respect is also due to scholars as well.

Adab demands such respect to scholars, because it is they who are the heirs to the Prophets. Children should learn from our example to honor and esteem scholars, never to act in an improper or unseemly manner in their presence, and to speak softly when they are in the room. At all times, scholars should be treated with courtesy and politeness.

Yahya ibn Muadh spoke of the value of scholars thus: "Scholars are more merciful to the family of believers than mothers and fathers are to their children." When he was asked why he said this, he answered, "Mothers and fathers save their children from the physical fire in this world, but scholars save them from the eternal fire in the Hereafter."[17] This is one of the reasons why scholars deserve respect from us.

A Prophetic saying, related by Ubada ibn al-Samit, states, "One who does not respect their elders, one who does not show sympathy and compassion for children, and one who does not know the value of scholars is not of us."[18] In another hadith the Prophet said, "A person who acquires knowledge merely so that they will be praised in front of scholars, or to argue with the ignorant, or to win the admiration of people is bound for Hell."[19]

As for the proper behavior for children toward scholars, Ibn Abbas related an experience he had as a child with one of the Companions: "When God's Messenger passed away, I asked a man from the Ansar, 'Come, I want to go and learn from the Companions of the Prophet because there are many here now.' The man replied, 'I am surprised at you, Ibn Abbas! Do you imagine that anyone will be in need of you (i.e. your knowledge) while the Companions of God's Messenger are still among us?' Then he left. I went to the Companions alone and asked them some questions. When I learned that a particular hadith had been related by someone, I would go to that person's house. If he were sleeping, I would use my cloak as a pillow and lie down in front of his door to wait; the wind would blow dust over me (while waiting there in patience). The man would come out and he would see me, usually addressing me, 'O cousin of the Prophet! What is wrong, why are you lying here? If you had sent word to me, I would have come to you!' (And in return) I would answer, 'No, it is more appropriate that I come to you.' I would then ask this Companion about the hadith. Later, one day when I was surrounded by people (and teaching them what I had learned), that same man from the Ansar came and saw that I was being asked questions. He said, 'This youth is more intelligent than I.'"[20]

The following example is another good example of the proper behavior of the children of the Companions towards the scholars: Said ibn al-Musayyab used to pray two *rakat*s of prayer and then sit down. The children of the Companions would gather around him, but no one would say anything or ask any questions until after he had recited a hadith for them. Then they would ask him questions.[21]

Hasan al-Basri likewise warned his son to practice *adab* with scholars, reminding him, "My child! When you sit with scholars, listen more than you speak. Just as you have learned to speak well, now learn to listen well. Until the scholar stops speaking—no matter how long he may speak—do not interrupt him!"

TEACHER ETIQUETTE

Just as the *adab* of teaching and learning applies to students of all kinds of knowledge, not only religious knowledge, all teachers, no matter what their subject, should practice *adab* in their duties. The following are some guidelines for teachers:

1. A teacher should be up to date on the latest information and developments in their field and always come to class well prepared.

2. A teacher should explain the topic at a level the students will understand, thus not destroying their motivation by making them feel it is too difficult.

3. A teacher should live an exemplary life which inspires respect in terms of their behavior, words, lifestyle, and morals. "Respect cannot be forced, it can only be given." Teachers who constantly scold their students, demand respect from them, and try to force it instead of inspiring it are not only the least beloved teachers, they are also the least effective.

4. A teacher should always strive to love teaching and to communicate their knowledge in the best way possible.

5. A teacher should approach students with the same compassion as a parent, not indulging hard workers, or belittling or putting down lazy students.

6. Students' faults should not be pointed out and listed in front of their friends in order to humiliate them; teaching requires tolerance and a forgiving nature.

7. When necessary, a teacher should listen to students to share their problems, give them support, and assist them. At the same time, they should be careful not to become so familiar and casual with the students that they lower the dignity of the pursuit of knowledge.

8. Grades should not be held over students' heads as a threat and a teacher must be impartial in assigning grades.

9. Teachers must avoid accepting expensive gifts, lavish dinner parties, or other such offers made by the families of students to safeguard the honor and integrity of their office.

STUDENT ETIQUETTE

Clear, concise rules are required for a child's moral education, character and values to develop properly and to ensure academic success. If this foundation is laid both at home and in the student–teacher relationship, the classroom environment becomes more enjoyable and positive. For this reason the most essential rules will be listed here:

1. Honesty: This is one of the most basic and critical corner-stones of communal life at any level. Lying, cheating, copying the work of others, stealing, or using things without permission must not be tolerated at school; indeed, they are unacceptable in every segment of society.

2. Courtesy: This is the outer expression of basic respect for oneself and others. Therefore, students must be held responsible for their choice of words or the tone of their voice. The same polite behavior and courtesy that they owe to their elders they also owe to their peers; that is, students need to be courteous to one another.

3. Social relationships: Students need to be taught to avoid insulting or using vulgar terms of address or styles of communication with one another. They must not forget that it is bad behavior to belittle, ridicule, or taunt other students, or to form cliques. Students should be admonished and warned about such behavior on a regular basis so they will take it seriously, thus learning to be careful about how they joke or tease others.

4. Personal care: This is an important mark of a person with excellent character. Children must learn to pay attention to personal cleanliness and bathe daily. As they grow, physical cleanliness becomes more and more important, and they should be aware of this. Hygiene is the most effective way to stay healthy and avoid contagious illnesses (which are often rife in school environments). So students should remember to wash their hands with soap before and after meals and before and after using the restroom.

PRACTICING GOOD CONDUCT
IN THE FAMILY

Good character is not only taught but can also be caught. Being a person of good character can best be achieved by learning what is good and bad, observing the limits set by God in the Scripture, witnessing good conduct in daily life, and emulating personal examples. To this end, modeling good character, especially in the family, is essential in raising children with character.

Morality, manners, and social life are learned in the family first. A healthy, ordered family life is necessary, as love and respect can be witnessed best in such a family. Good character characteristics can be gained and developed in the family. A child who learns respect for the grandmother and grandfather, obedience to the father and mother, and decent behavior toward those of their own generation within the family will have these positive traits when they enter society at large.

With that introduction, let us take a look at good conduct in the family.

TREATING CHILDREN WITH COMPASSION

As is well known, daily prayers and fasting are among the most essential pillars of our faith. But in both these practices, we can clearly see compassion for children, both in the religious guidelines and in the example of the Prophet's life. While performing daily prayers has the highest priority in worship for the Prophet, he never refrained from being kind to children, even while praying or leading the congregational prayers. For example, the Prophet's granddaughter Umama would come to the mosque to play and climb on the Prophet's shoulders and back as he led the prayers. When he went to prostrate he put the child down, and when he straightened up he took her up on his shoulders again.[22] Sometimes he wished to lengthen the congregational prayers, but if he heard a child crying at the back of the mosque, he would change his plans and shorten the prayers out of compassion for the child and the feelings of the mother.[23]

There is another important narration which demonstrates clearly the extent of Prophet Muhammad's consideration for children. This was conveyed by 'Abdullah ibn Shaddad from his father: "God's Messenger came to us for the evening prayers one day. He carried one of his grandchildren, Hasan or Husayn. He put the child on the floor and went to the front (to lead us). Then he recited the opening *takbir* and began the prayers. During the prayer, he stayed prostrated for a long time. (Since it was so long) I picked up my head and looked. What did I see! A child had climbed on the Prophet's back while he was prostrating, and was sitting there. Immediately I prostrated again. When the prayers had finished, the people asked him, 'O Messenger of God! The prostration was so long, we thought something had happened to you, or perhaps you were receiving revelation?' He answered, 'No! Neither of these things happened. My child had climbed on my back. I thought it inappropriate to hurry him to get off before he was ready to (I waited until he got down before continuing).'"[24]

This compassion for children in Islam is not limited to prayer times. When we look at fasting (in the month of Ramadan, when all believers are required to fast), there are important exceptions for mothers and children. For example, as a mercy from God to women and their children, pregnant or nursing mothers are given legal allowance not to fast.[25]

Again, another important principle is that children under the age of puberty are not obligated to observe the fast. They are also exempted from the obligation of the other acts of worship until they reach the age of puberty and discretion.[26] Normally this age is considered to be fifteen years old.[27]

One of the most serious wrongs that can be done to a child is for the parents to curse the child—even if it only happens "by mistake" due to impatience on a rare occasion. The danger of this type of curse is that even when the bad words slip out of a person's mouth, they are a form of prayer. Jabir relates, "The Messenger said, 'Do not pray against your own souls, do not pray against your children, do not pray against your servants. Do not even pray against your possessions. For if you pray at the time when prayers are accepted, God may accept your prayer."[28]

Once in a war zone, some children were caught between the enemy lines and were killed. When the Prophet heard about this, he was grief-stricken. The solders, seeing this, asked him, "O Messenger of God, why are you so disconsolate? Were not these children of the enemies of God?" He answered, "Even if they were children of the enemy, they were human beings. Weren't the most pious among you the children of the enemy at one point? You must take the utmost care never to kill children. By God every life is created with a nature that is open to faith and Islam."[29]

One day when he was being affectionate to his grandchildren, a Bedouin came into the Prophet's presence. When this man, who was devoid of compassion for his children, saw the scene, he could not hide his surprise and said, "I have ten children, and I have never kissed any of them." The Prophet answered, "If God Almighty has extracted all the mercy from your heart, what can I do? Those who have no mercy will be shown none."[30]

Anas ibn Malik recounted, "The Prophet used to join us children and, smiling, banter with us."[31] Anas also recalled, "I served God's Messenger for ten years. I swear before God, he never once lost his patience with me. He never asked me, 'Why did you do that? You should have done it another way."[32]

RESPECT

The dictionary definition of "respect" includes "the feeling that arises from holding someone in high esteem which inspires conduct that shows the person they are valued"; "valuing someone and desiring not to disappoint them"; "a type of love which causes one to act with care and propriety around someone, and treat them with altruism." Thus, the meaning of respect is connected with love, which explains why the most common word occurring alongside "respect" is "love." The bonds of brotherhood between members of a community are strengthened by love and respect. The secret of success also lies in loving and respecting others.

It is a sign of respect to the Creator when we respect and love other people simply because they are human. To love only those who think as we do is not sincere love for humankind; it is self-serving, and can even be a form of idolatry of the self. Likewise, it is not true respect to show deference to people only according to their rank or position. One who does not love everyone does not deserve to be loved; if one is constantly reviling the poor and unfortunate, they will lose the right to expect love and respect from others. According to a narration from Abu Musa, the Prophet said, "To show respect to an old Muslim with white hair, to a *hafiz* (a person who has memorized the Qur'an) as long as they recite and live by the Qur'an, or to a righteous ruler all manifest true respect for God."[33]

It is part of *adab* to let older people speak before young people in daily conversations or situations. The following hadith exemplifies this tradition. Abu Yahya of the Ansar related, "Abdur Rahman ibn Sahl went with Muhayyisa ibn Mas'ud to Haybar. They separated from one another to take care of their individual business. Then they came to Medina. Abdur Rahman and Muhayyisa, the sons of Mas'ud, went into the Prophet's presence. When Abdur Rahman wanted to talk, God's Messenger told him, 'Let older people speak.' For Abdur Rahman was the youngest of the brothers."[34] Therefore it is important to give elders the chance to speak first, out of respect for their experience and wisdom. Younger people should speak when spoken to or when asked a question, instead of monopolizing the conversation.

Lastly, Samura ibn Jundab, a Companion who was a child during the Prophet's life, recalls the following: "I was a child during the time of the Prophet and I memorized whatever I heard when he was teaching. The only thing that kept me from speaking in the gatherings was that there were older people there."

Treating the Elderly with Respect

In Islam, the general rule is that those who are older than us should be respected, and those who are younger than us should be loved. In addition, it is commendable to care for those who have fallen on hard times. In fact, God's help reaches us through those people who need our help; our subsistence and sustenance may be increased for the sake of the adults and children whom we support.[35]

The basic rule of respect for elders is even more important between family members. An example is the extra respect due to mothers and fathers. It is not proper to call our parents by their first names. Below are some of the hadith of the Prophet on this topic:

"If any young person shows respect to an older person because of the age difference, God will appoint someone to show him similar respect when he himself grows old."[36] This hadith informs us that young people will be rewarded for respecting elders and will be shown respect as they themselves grow old. Young people who perceive the elderly as a burden should think about this.

"Those who do not show mercy to younger people or show respect to older people are not of us."[37] This hadith summarizes the relationship between younger and older people in a clear and succinct manner. The Prophet said, "To have respect for an older Muslim with graying hair shows one has respect for God."[38]

In order to develop feelings of respect towards elders the following issues should be focused on:

1. In all the family business of a household, the father and mother should be considered the authorities. This behavior

encourages the internalization of respect for elders. A hadith says, "Blessings are to be found next to your elders."[39]

2. The respect and reverence shown by parents to their own mother and father (i.e., the children's grandparents) serve as a great lesson to the children. If a child's mother and father are always loving and compassionate, the child will be more aware of the duty and obligation to respect their parents and other elders. People develop this awareness over a long time and through habit. A child needs to see how to obey and respect elders over and over again to absorb this lesson. Otherwise it would be difficult—sometimes even impossible—to expect the desired result to come by simply teaching rules that are not practiced. God's Messenger expressed the critical need in a society for young people to maintain respectful attitudes and behavior toward those who are older than themselves: "If there were not white-haired elders, suckling babies, and grazing animals among you, calamities would have rained down on you like a flood."[40]

Kissing the Hands of the Elderly and Esteemed People

We show our respect for older persons and scholars by kissing their hands. We know from narrations that the Companions kissed the hand of the Prophet.[41] God's Messenger said, "Our elders are a blessing. Those who do not respect elders and show compassion for youths are not of us."[42] Children usually kiss the hands of all their elders; after puberty, young people should kiss the hands of their mothers, fathers, grandparents, aunts and uncles, and older siblings.

It is accepted that kissing the hands of Islamic scholars is *mubah*, or "acceptable," if it is done out of respect or piety, but it is unacceptable to kiss someone's hand for worldly reasons. Just as it is forbidden for members of the opposite sex to hold hands in

Islam, it is also objectionable to engage in flattery or sycophancy, or to bow before others. There is some disagreement regarding whether a son-in-law should kiss the hand of his mother-in-law or a daughter-in-law the hand of her father-in-law. There is no harm in kissing the hands of elderly women as a sign of respect. What is important here is that kissing a person's hand is performed as a sign of respect.

While heeding the warning of God's Messenger, "Do not stand up as the Persians stand up for each other," the elder should not desire to have his or her hand kissed, but the youth should try to kiss the hand of the elder person; an older person should not expect a show of respect, but the younger should not neglect to do so. It is also to be noted here that members of various communities would come and ask the Prophet questions and he would answer all their questions. Tirmidhi relates that two people of the Jewish community in Medina came to ask the Messenger a question and they kissed his hand.[43]

To show respect for scholars and holy people, and so on, one may kiss their hands or perform *musafaha*[44] with them. There is no objection either way, for we should respect real knowledge and God-consciousness. However, it would be wrong for a person to consider themselves to be holy and thus expect their hand to be kissed. It is also permissible for the hands of other older people to be kissed out of respect for their piety. But prostrating in front of scholars or other people is not permissible. To do so, or allowing this to be done, is a sin as it borders on a kind of idol worship. For this reason Muslims should not perform such actions.

PROPER ATTITUDES TOWARDS PARENTS

W e will now examine the Qur'anic teachings on the *adab* toward parents. In the Qur'an God commands, *"Your Lord has decreed that you worship none but Him alone, and treat parents with the best of kindness..."* (Isra 17:23). It is notable that two of the central themes of the Qur'an are mentioned one after the other. The first is *tawhid* (divinity, God's Oneness and Absolute Unity), which is the most important theme of the Qur'an. Immediately after *tawhid*, God decrees that we must treat our parents well. "Treating parents well" is further explained in the Qur'an (17:23–24) with five main principles. If one or both of (your parents) grows old and is still with you:

1. Do not be impatient when caring for them.
2. Do not reprove them.
3. Speak to them in a gentle, endearing manner.
4. Lower the *"wing of humility"* to them.
5. Pray for them thus: *"My Lord, have mercy on them in the way that they cared for me in childhood (and reward them for the way they cared for me and raised me)."*

Abu Baddah al-Tujibi recounts that he asked Said ibn al-Musayyab, "I have learned all the verses regarding goodness to parents. But there is one I do not understand. What does '*address them in gracious words*' mean?" The scholar answered, "This means that you should speak to them as an employee speaks to the employer, and not be harsh to them." (As with everything in Islam, intention is also extremely important.) Parents sacrifice their lives lovingly for their children, and what the child must do is to show sincere respect for the parent, to serve them willingly, and to try to gain their approval. They should always say gentle and endearing words to their parents. After setting these principles for how children should treat their parents, God also warns those who insincerely or unwillingly care for their parents that their inner situation is not hidden from Him: *"Your Lord best knows what is in your souls (in respect of all matters, including what you think of your parents). If you are righteous (in your thoughts and deeds), then surely He is All-Forgiving to those who turn to Him in humble contrition"* (Isra 17:25).

God Almighty further says in the Qur'an, *"We have enjoined on human in respect of his parents: his mother bore him in strain upon strain, and his weaning was in two years. (So, O human,) be thankful to Me and to your parents. To Me is the final homecoming"* (Luqman 31:14). This verse orders that we treat our parents well, and mentions the physical hardships that mothers undergo such as pregnancy, childbirth, and nursing, as well as the emotional bond between mothers and children during the first years of life. The verse then goes on to enumerate the *adab* or principles of etiquette that one must use towards parents:

> [Revere your parents;] but if they strive with you to make you associate with Me something of which you certainly have no knowledge (and which is absolutely contrary to the Knowledge), do not obey them. Even then, treat them with kindness and due consideration in respect of (the life of) this world. Follow the way of him who has turned to Me with utmost sincerity and committed himself to seeking My approval. Then, (O all human beings,) to Me is your return, and then I will make you understand all that you were doing (and call you to account). (Luqman 31:15)

This section of the Qur'an shows that we are to care for the needs of our parents and treat them with gentleness and respect, even if they are not Muslims. Islamic scholars pay great attention to the interpretation of the following sentence: *"treat them with kindness and due consideration in respect of (the life of) this world."* Generally, it is agreed that one should spend time with parents, seeing to all their needs, such as food, clothing, shelter, and so on. We should never speak harshly or cruelly to our parents, but ensure that their medical needs have been provided for and assist them in all they require in this life. This is confirmed by the following episode from the time of the Prophet:

Abu Bakr's daughter Asma relates: "My mother, who was still an unbeliever, came to me. (Unsure of how to treat her,) I asked God's Messenger, 'My mother has come to see me; she wants to talk to me. Should I be kind to her?' God's Messenger answered, 'Yes, show her the respect and kindness she deserves.'"[45]

The following verse, just like the fourteenth verse of Sura Luqman, states that the weaning period for a child is two years and refers to the pregnancy and nursing of a child as consisting of thirty months:

> Now (among the good deeds) We have enjoined on human is the best treatment towards his parents. His mother bore him in pain, and in pain did she give him birth. The bearing of him and suckling of him (until weaned) is thirty months.... (Ahqaf 46:15)

The verses we have examined so far emphasize the difficulty that mothers undergo in pregnancy, birth, and nursing as the basic reason for the order to treat one's parents well. If we make some effort to understand more deeply, there are more important insights to be gained. We can see that the verse at hand begins with the same command that is found in the fourteenth verse of Sura Luqman; however, it then continues along quite different guidelines. This difference, as I will attempt to explain, takes the form of a prayer, which includes four parts:

> When he has reached full manhood and forty years of age, he says, 'My Lord! Arouse me so that I may be thankful for all Your favors (life, health, sustenance, faith, submission, and more) which You have bestowed on me and on my parents, and so that I may do good, righteous deeds with which You will be pleased, and grant me righteous offspring (so that they treat me righteously, as I treat my parents). I have turned to You, and I am one of those who have submitted to You.' (Ahqaf 46:15)

Adults can use this prayer to ask for God's mercy and blessings, for a closer bond with God, and a peaceful and balanced social life. Ibn Abbas said he heard the Prophet say, "Whoever looks at his mother or father with mercy, God grants him the reward (for that gaze which will be the same) for a valid *hajj*."[46]

In connection with not upsetting or disobeying one's father, Ibn Abbas reported that the Messenger of God, peace and blessings be upon him, said, "When a father looks at his child and the child makes the father happy, the child is given as much reward as if he or she has freed a slave."[47] Abu'd Darda heard the Prophet say, "The father is a major door into Heaven. A person can choose to abandon this door or choose to protect it (keep it open)."[48] Another important hadith on the topic of pleasing fathers is conveyed by 'Abdullah ibn Amr ibn al-As: "The Prophet said, 'The pleasure of God lies in pleasing one's father and God's displeasure lies in the father's displeasure.'"[49]

Adult children can still gain blessings in the name of their parents after they have passed on, according to God's word. A hadith explains this:

Abu Usayd Malik ibn Rabi'a al-Saidi recounts that a man asked the Prophet, "O Messenger of God, after my mother and father are gone, is it still possible for me to do good for them? What can I do for them?" The Messenger replied, "Yes, you can." He went on to advise us to:

1. Pray for them, ask God to forgive them,
2. Carry out their last will and testament,
3. Remember to visit our parents' relatives,
4. Send gifts to our parents' friends.[50]

God's Messenger also warned those who did not visit their parents or care for them while they are still alive.

Abu Hurayra related the following hadith of the Prophet: "Woe to him, woe to him, woe to him!" said the Prophet. When they asked, "Woe to whom?" he gave this explanation: "Woe to the one who has one or both of his parents grow old with him, and (still) cannot make it to heaven."[51]

CARE OF KIN

The Islamic term used for the care of kin is *sila al-rahm* which encompasses visiting one's parents and relatives, asking after their welfare, and making them happy. Islam gives importance to relationships with people, particularly the mother and father and then other close relatives. Visiting them should become a principle in one's life.

Khalid ibn Zayd (Abu Ayyub al-Ansari) narrated an event in which a man came and asked the Prophet, "O Messenger of God, can you tell me an act of worship that will help me enter Heaven?" God's Messenger replied thus, "Worshipping God, not associating any partners with Him, performing the daily prayers, giving to charity, and visiting your relatives."[52]

This hadith emphasizes the importance of *sila al-rahm*, stating that such actions can help Muslims go to Heaven. But *sila al-rahm* means more than just visiting relatives; it also includes taking care of their needs and always including them when doing something helpful (like giving charity). The fact that this is mentioned directly after the prescribed acts of worship, such as daily prayers and charity, shows the great importance given to *sila al-rahm* in Islam. For this reason, some Islamic scholars hold that such behavior is *wajib*, or necessary, for believers, and they consider it to be a great sin to neglect or refuse these duties. Indeed, in the Qur'an God commands:

> O humankind! In due reverence for your Lord, keep from disobedience to Him Who created you from a single human self, and from it created its mate, and from the pair of them scattered abroad a multitude of men and women. In due reverence for God, keep from disobedience to Him in Whose name you

make demands of one another, and (duly observe) the rights of the wombs (i.e. of kinship, thus observing piety in your relations with God and with human beings). God is ever watchful over you. (Nisa 4:1)

In the verse above, as well as the following verse, God's Word charges us to maintain the bond of family ties, look after relatives and never allow these relationships to be severed:

And those who unite the bonds God has commanded to be joined (among kin as a requirement of blood relationship, and among people as required by human social interdependence), and stand in awe of their Lord, and fearful of (facing) the most evil reckoning... But those who break God's covenant after its solemn binding, and sever the bonds God commanded to be joined, and cause disorder and corruption on the earth—such are those on whom there is a curse (exclusion from God's mercy), and for them there is the most evil abode. (Ra'd 13:20, 25)

There are differences of opinion as to how far the designation of "relative" extends, or who, exactly, is meant by these verses and hadith. According to some, relatives are close relatives with whom marriage is forbidden; according to others, the word's meaning is those relatives close enough to have rights to inheritance. Still other scholars believe that the word *rahm* in the verse is inclusive of all relatives, even if they are distant relatives. In terms of social life the latter view is the most helpful.

Since it has been commanded by God and His Messenger Prophet Muhammad, peace and blessings be upon him, to visit and care for relatives, it would be appropriate here to examine how this should be done. There are certain "degrees" of *sila al-rahm*:

1. The absolute minimum is to speak kindly to relatives and be amiable when talking to them, to greet them when we encounter them, to ask after their well-being, and to always think positively about them and want the best for them.

2. The second level is to go and visit them and to come to their aid in various circumstances. Such actions are a more physical way of serving our relatives. This is especially important as our relatives get older and need someone to assist them with things they can no longer do for themselves.

3. The third and most important level of *sila al-rahm* is to give one's relatives financial and material support.

There are exceptional circumstances, such as when someone is too poor to support their relatives materially. But the Muslim who is well-off cannot be said to have completed the duties of *sila al-rahm* simply by visiting and asking after their relatives. For such a person, these duties include financial support, as much as they can afford, for less well-off relatives. This support can be in the form of giving them a regular amount of money, or providing them with the things they need. This is what is meant by "looking after and caring for relatives" in Islam; a good Muslim should carry out all of the above three "degrees" of support to the best of their ability. Otherwise, if they neglect to carry out those duties that are in their power, they will be held accountable. We must keep in mind the punishment for those who neglect these duties given in the above Qur'anic verse. Our Prophet also said, "Every Friday night each person's deeds are presented to God; only those who neglect *sila al-rahm* will have their deeds denied."[53]

Prophet Muhammad, peace and blessings be upon him, spoke of this topic in another hadith, proclaiming that faith in God and in the Last Day requires looking after one's relatives.[54] The Prophet said that God's mercy is on those whom God judges to be taking good care of their families and those who take care to maintain blood ties. Conversely, God curses anyone who makes no effort to maintain their relationships with their relatives.[55]

There are also other warnings that state that those who cut ties with their relatives will be punished. The Prophet declared that such people will not be admitted to Paradise.[56] He also taught that only those who take good care of their relatives will be granted longer life and more abundance,[57] and that one who gives financial help to relatives will be rewarded twice, both for helping family and for giving to charity.[58]

The term *relatives* usually implies close relations such as immediate family, cousins, aunts or uncles. There are special benefits in treating these relatives well. The Messenger of God said, "An aunt is like another mother."[59] Likewise, an uncle is like another father. It is only natural that as part of good morality such close family members have certain rights on us. Among these rights, paying visits is of particular importance. As explained below, the general rule is that one should visit close relations first on holidays, and then occasionally at other times, if possible bringing gifts.

Visiting strengthens the bond of love between relatives, and puts an end to estrangement. It allows people to share their sorrows and joys, and to help one another through difficult times. In particular, the elderly need to spend their final years in peace and happiness in the bosom of their family, knowing they are loved and cared for.

There is another consideration that should be taken into account when examining the subject of *sila al-rahm*. One should not expect anything in return; in this context, this means that we must not only look after the relatives with whom we are already close, but we should also attend to our duties toward those who have severed ties with us. The Prophet said, "One who simply returns good with good is not living the full meaning of 'caring for relatives.' True care means to care for the relation who has not shown us any regard."[60] In fact this is a general principle—we should always think carefully and choose the good action in every situation. It is not correct to look after the well-being of those in need when one is weak and powerless but to change one's conduct when wealth and power increase. This situation is one among the thousands of layers of meaning in the following Qur'anic verse:

But is it to be expected of you (O hypocritical ones), that you will break your promise and turn away (from God's commandments), and cause disorder and corruption in the land, and sever the ties of kinship? Such are they whom God has cursed (excluded from His mercy), and so He has made them deaf and blinded their eyes (to the truth). (Muhammad 47:22–3)

As a final point, I wish to point out a general principle found in a hadith of the Prophet. Being fallible humans, we may sometimes let bad words slip, especially when we are agitated and angry. There is a striking hadith about this: Ibn Amr ibn al-As relates the following words of Prophet Muhammad, peace and blessings be upon him: "One of the greatest sins is to curse one's parents." Those with him asked, "Would any person curse their own parents?" The Messenger answered, "Yes! If anyone curses the parent of another person, as that person will then curse their parent in return, it is as if he has cursed his own parent!"[61]

JEALOUSY AND RIVALRY
AMONG SIBLINGS

Quarreling among siblings may often be a result of their ages or stages of development. For example, the endless "why?" questions of a three-year-old may be intolerable for a ten-year-old sister or brother. Or, a small child who likes to sit quietly and play with their toys alone may naturally express annoyance when confronted by a headstrong adolescent sibling.

Another basic cause of contention is rivalry and jealousy among siblings. After all, jealousy has been a human condition since the beginning of time. Some people are mature and fully grown, but still retain anger and resentment against those close to them. Since they have not been able to get over their childhood jealousy, feelings of resentment and envy have grown and changed shape; these could even be a threat to the community.

Sibling rivalry arises from a desire to compete for the affection of the parents. If one child is shown a great deal of affection by the parents, the other children will be jealous. But children do not demonstrate feelings of jealousy in a direct manner. A jealous child may feign affection toward their sibling. Such a child will often be inclined to try to hurt the brother or sister when no one else is around.

In the famous story in the Qur'an about Joseph, Joseph's brothers tried to harm him, spurred on by jealousy. The Qur'an says, *"Assuredly, in (this account of) Joseph and his brothers there are many signs (messages) for seekers of truth"* (Yusuf 12:7).

As is well known, Prophet Jacob fathered twelve sons. However, Jacob discerned great potential in Joseph and therefore he paid greater attention to Joseph. Because this was obvious, the other brothers' jealousy grew against Joseph. One night Joseph had a dream. When he woke he said to his father, "*O my father! I saw in a dream eleven stars, as well as the sun and the moon: I saw them prostrating themselves before me*" (Yusuf 12:4). Jacob thought about this dream, and he believed it meant God would give Joseph every kind of opportunity, bestowed on him a high level of honor and renown, and make him an important leader. Aware of the feelings of the other brothers toward Joseph, Jacob feared they would try to harm him. So he told him, "*O my son! Do not relate your dream to your brothers, lest (out of envy) they devise a scheme against you. For Satan is a manifest enemy to humankind (and can incite them to do such a thing)*" (Yusuf 12:5). The Qur'an goes on to describe the plan the brothers hatched, a terrible example of just how far jealousy between siblings can go:

> When they (the brothers addressing one another) said, "Joseph and his brother are indeed more loved by our father than we are, even though we are a powerful band (of greater use to him). Surely, our father is manifestly mistaken." (One of them said:) "Kill Joseph, or cast him out in some distant land so that your father's attention should turn only to you, and after that you may again become righteous people." (Yusuf 12:8–9)

It is the duty of parents to recognize when a child is jealous, and watch for how it will be expressed. From this aspect, keeping tabs on the relations between siblings and keeping their bickering under control can be a very difficult task for a family.

Undeniably, jealousy is an emotion that is embedded in human nature. The important thing is to prevent this negative element from causing damage to children and their environment. The way to do this is to channel these tendencies toward the positive with self-discipline. It is difficult to put forward any general, practically feasible solutions for such situations, as they are very sensitive and complex. It is of course necessary, in principle, for parents to listen to children, try to understand the reasons for their behavior, and examine their own attitudes and approaches. Parents should develop the ability to see situations and conditions from their children's perspective.

Other things parents can do to neutralize jealousy are to prepare games that will help children spend their physical and emotional energy in positive ways and to praise children when they get along well and have fun together. Here are a few more tips:

1. Avoid incorrect educational methods. For example, do not always take the part of the younger sibling or automatically blame the older sibling. Often if you intervene just to "save" the younger child, it gives rise to contention between them without you realizing it. Further, you may not know whether it was actually the older child who instigated the problem or not. Accordingly, sensitivity and attention are necessary if we are to treat children equally. It is also good to give them a chance to solve their own problems; tell them you trust them to do so.

2. Be sure to spend equal amounts of time with each child every day. If one is jealous of the other's time, tell them that you want to be with each child and their turn will come.

3. Take care to make a distinction between siblings, and not to hold the others responsible when only one is doing something wrong.

4. Avoid giving different treatment to girls and boys, giving more importance to one or the other or being more proud of one or the other. For example, parents may have a son after many daughters or a daughter after many sons; in such situations they tend to love this youngest more or show more tolerance toward them. This naturally promotes problems between the children.

RESPECTING PRIVACY AT HOME

Members of the family should respect the sanctity of each other's privacy in the family. The *adab* of asking for permission before entering a room is especially important for privacy in home life, and this *adab* can be gained and developed with practice.

According to the Qur'an, mothers and fathers should train their children to ask for permission and they should follow a progressive pedagogical method to this end. Until adolescence, children should knock and wait for permission before entering the room of their parents, at three particular times of the day. These are times when the mother and father need privacy because they may be wearing nightclothes. The private times are before dawn, in the early afternoon, when they may be sleeping, and after the night prayers. In the Qur'an God says:

> O you who believe! Let those whom your right hands possess (as slaves), as well as those of you (your children) who have not yet reached puberty, ask for your permission (before they come into your private room) at three times (of the day)—before the Morning Prayer, and when you lay aside your garments in the middle of the day for rest, and after the Night Prayer. These are your three times of privacy. Beyond these occasions, there is no blame on you nor on them if they come in without permission—they are bound to move about you, some of you attending on others. Thus God makes clear for you (the instructions in) the Revelations. God is All-Knowing, All-Wise. (Nur 24:58)

When children reach maturity, they should knock and wait for permission before entering any room when the door is closed, be it in their own home or someone else's. The following verse makes this clear:

> And when your children reach puberty, let them ask you for permission (whenever they want to enter your private room), even as those (who have already reached the same age) before them ask for it. Thus God makes clear for you (the instructions in) His revelations. God is All-Knowing, All-Wise. (Nur 24:59)

SLEEP

Regular sleep is necessary for the purpose of rest and rejuvenation. On average, we spend one third of our day sleeping. Such a large part of daily life should be examined to make sure that this time is spent in the right way and not carelessly. When the fruitful lives of productive people are examined, we can see that they worked much and slept little. Thus, it follows that we should sleep only as much as necessity dictates. Those who sleep less actually have more energy than those who sleep too much, and are more effective and outgoing. People who sleep little are more likely to be happy with themselves and their life, and to have better interactions with the outside world. From the active person's perspective, time spent sleeping is lost time. It is obvious that reducing the time spent sleeping will increase the time we have to do things that matter in life. So, once again, we should approach our sleeping and waking consciously and with care.

1. Before going to bed we should make ablutions. There is a hadith related by Abu Umama that the Prophet said, "Whoever enters the bed with ablutions and engages in remembrance of God until falling asleep, and then wakes up at some hour of the night and asks God for something either material or eternal, God will certainly give it to him."[62]

2. It is *Sunna*, to clean our teeth before bed and upon waking. The Messenger also cleaned his teeth when he woke up during the night to pray.[63] In addition, he would clean his teeth and take ablutions before lying down, whether at night or in the daytime.[64]

3. When going to bed for the night, we should intend to wake up during the night and pray. The Prophet said, "I recommend that you get up at night. For the saints who lived before you used this as a path to get close to God, to save themselves from sin, to atone for wrongs, and to protect the body from illness."[65] In another hadith he said, "May God extend His bounteous mercy to the man who gets up at night to pray, and wakes up his wife also, and if she does not get up, pours water on her face. May God extend His bounteous mercy to the woman who gets up at night to pray and wakes up her husband, and if he does not get up, pours water on his face."[66]

4. Someone who is unsure whether or not they can wake up at night should perform the three rakat *witr* prayer before going to bed, though its preferable time is after the supererogatory prayer of *tahajjud* which is performed at night. For the Prophet said, "Whoever is afraid he cannot get up at the end of the night to pray *witr*, let him do it at the beginning of the night. Whoever hopes to wake up at the end of the night, let him pray *witr* at the end of the night (before the time comes for the obligatory morning prayer). For prayers at the end of the night are acceptable and pleasing to God (since both night and day angels are gathered together ready to bring mercy.) So it is more virtuous to pray at the end of the night."[67]

5. If you have trouble sleeping, the Prophet made the following suggestion. One day, Khalid ibn Walid al-Makhzumi said to the Prophet, "O God's Messenger, last night I could not sleep at all!" The Prophet told him, "When you enter your bed say this prayer: 'O Lord of the seven heavens and everything else they shade! O Lord of the worlds and everything else they contain! O Lord and Creator of satans and all the creatures they have led astray! Safeguard me against the evil of all these creatures, so that none may

descend upon me, nor attack me. One whom You protect is mighty. Your praise is exalted, there is no deity but You, the only deity is You."[68]

6. When lying down, recite Suras Falaq and Nas. According to a narration from Aisha, the Prophet would read these as well as Sura Ikhlas when he came to bed, and then wipe his face and body with his hands three times. He told her to read these suras to him when he was unwell.[69]

We should also pay attention to the following things when we get up in the morning:

1. Try to go to bed early and wake up early.
2. Mention God when you wake up.
3. Wear something appropriate to your situation.
4. Take your ablutions and do your morning prayer immediately after getting up.
5. Eat from the permissible bounties God provides.
6. Have complete trust in God.
7. Thank God for all the blessings He has given you.
8. Earn your living in an upright way (not by cheating others, etc.).

Finally, there is a beautiful prayer that it is recommended to read in the morning. Make your intention for the day (for example, "I am going to work in an upright, honest way for my own and my family's sustenance, not to depend on another's generosity nor get into debt, to worship God and please Him, and to serve people.") Then, as you leave the house, say, "In God's Name (I leave my home), and I depend on and trust God. Only God Almighty can grant power and strength (in every way.)"[70]

CLEANLINESS

The Prophet said that "cleanliness is half of faith." Therefore, we should recognize the importance of both inward and outward cleanliness, and keep our living quarters and environment clean.

In Islam there is a great emphasis on cleanliness, both physical and spiritual. After the occasion of the first revelation of a verse of the Qur'an ("*Read!*"), the second verse to be revealed was a command about wearing clean clothing: "*O you cloaked one (who has preferred solitude)! Arise and warn! And declare your Lord's (indescribable and incomparable) greatness. And keep your clothing clean! Keep away from all pollution*" (Muddaththir 74:1–5).

The Islamic scholar Elmalili Hamdi Yazir interprets the word *siyab* (usually "clothing") in this verse to signify the "soul" and the "heart." Thus, he paraphrases the verse as "keep yourself and your heart clean from sin and unrighteousness, stay away from unclean feelings that will ruin your good deeds, and clothe yourself in good morality so that your good works may be acceptable." But Yazir also sees no problem with a literal understanding of the verse, directly referring to physical and outward cleanliness, as well. Thus, it is highly likely that the verse is also a commandment to keep the body and its garments clean.[71]

It is clear that this responsibility—to keep oneself clean, both from outward impurities as well as from sins, like ascribing partners to God, rebellion against God, hypocrisy, and so on—is a moral obligation demanded by Islam. Both types of uncleanness are mentioned together in another Qur'anic verse: "*Surely God loves those who turn to Him in sincere repentance (of past sins and errors) and He loves those who cleanse themselves*" (Baqara 2:222).

The first requirement for deserving God's love, entering His Presence, and being His servant is cleanliness. It is the first thing we must do to put ourselves in the correct state for performing obligatory daily prayers, which are the "ascension of the believer." In the following verse God decrees performing ablution or taking a bath for this purpose:

> O you who believe! When you rise up for the Prayer, (if you have no ablution) wash your faces and your hands up to (and including) the elbows, and lightly rub your heads (with water) and (wash) your feet up to (and including) the ankles. And if you are in the state of major ritual impurity (requiring total ablution), purify yourselves (by taking a bath).... (Maeda 5:6)

With this verse the ablutions before ritual prayers became obligatory and all Muslims wash their hands, faces, mouths, noses, ears, necks, and feet before each of the five daily prayers.

Just as we should keep our body and the clothes we wear clean, we also need to keep our living quarters and the places where we worship clean. The Qur'an says, "*O children of Adam! Dress cleanly and beautifully for every act of worship...*" (A'raf 7:31). God's Messenger made it an obligatory practice to bathe at least once a week (this was at a time when frequent bathing was uncommon).[72] He also instructed people to "keep your environment clean"[73] and urged them to maintain the shared community spaces as well. A hadith recounts his words on this subject: "Avoid two cursed things," he said, and when the Companions asked "What two things?" he replied, "Relieving oneself on the road where people pass by, or in a shady place (where people take a rest)."[74]

Prophet Muhammad, who was "the Living Qur'an" and who embodied Qur'anic morality, as with everything, was the best of examples in cleanliness. He was very careful about his own cleanliness and whenever he lay down or got up, day or night, he washed his mouth and nose, brushed his teeth[75] and made ablutions.[76] In particular he emphasized that cleaning the teeth is crucial not only for the health of our mouth, but also to please God[77]; moreover, he taught that the first thing a person should do on waking from sleep is to wash their hands.[78] He was also careful to dry his limbs on a towel after washing.[79] God's Messenger paid close attention to cleanliness throughout his life; he would wear clean, nice clothes whenever he out went in public, particularly to the mosque or to visit someone. He used pleasant scents and avoided eating onions, garlic or smelly foods before going out.

CLOTHING AND OUTER APPEARANCE

Wearing clean and tidy clothes is the *Sunna* of the Prophet. It should be kept in mind that dressing in such a way is not a display of vanity or arrogance for a person who has the means to dress well. In fact, God has made it clear that a person has the right to wear clothing that is befitting to the wealth they have been blessed with.

Awf ibn Malik relates from his father, "One day I came to God's Messenger wearing a coarse, cheap garment. He said to me, 'Have you no wealth?' I said, 'Yes, I have.' He asked, 'What kind of wealth?' I said, 'God has given me every kind of wealth: camels, cattle, flocks, horses, slaves.' He said, 'Then let the abundance of God's blessings be apparent on your person!'"[80] From other hadith we know that the Prophet wore his best clothing. He also had his Companions do likewise. The following narration not only mentions this, but also teaches that those with the responsibility of acting as representatives must dress particularly well. Ibn Abbas conveyed the following hadith: "It was when the Haruriyya (a branch of Khawarij) revolted. I went to Caliph Ali. He told me, 'Go to those people.' So I went and put on the best Yemeni garment. Then I came to them and they said, 'Welcome to you, Ibn Abbas! Why are you so dressed up?' I said, 'How could I be otherwise? I saw God's Messenger wearing the best clothing he has!'"[81]

It is also good *adab* to say a prayer the first time a new garment is worn, for the protection of God on the wearer. Abu Umama remembers, "Ibn Umar put on a new garment and prayed thus, 'Praise be to God, Who has given me clothing to cover my body and bring beauty to my life.' Then he added, 'I heard God's Messenger say, 'Whoever wears a new piece of clothing, and prays thus, will be under the protection and preservation of God both while he lives and after he dies.'"[82]

The Prophet also forbade Muslim men to wear silk clothing. Ali ibn Abu Talib explained, "One day God's Messenger took some silk in his right hand, and some gold in his left hand, and said, 'These two things are prohibited for my male followers.'" According to a similar hadith from Tirmidhi and Nasai, Abu Musa quoted him as saying, "Silk clothing and gold are forbidden for the men in my community, but allowed for the women."[83]

On the matter of outward appearance it is better to avoid broad generalizations concerning the issue of cutting hair so as not to cause any misunderstanding. It is best to mention the relevant hadith and comment on them briefly. Some reported sayings of the Prophet are as follows:

Anas ibn Malik reported that God's Messenger said, "He who has hair should honor it."[84] We honor our hair by combing it and keeping it tidy. The Prophet disliked disheveled hair. One should either comb the hair or have a short haircut which does not require much adornment. Ibn Umar narrated, "God's Messenger saw a boy whose head had been partly shaven. He forbade people to do this, saying, "Shave it all or leave it all."[85] Again, Ibn Umar tells us that God's Messenger prohibited believers from shaving part of the head and leaving the rest unshaven.[86]

The Prophet used to look after children's hair. As narrated by 'Abdullah, the son of Ja'far, God's Messenger came to visit them three days after the death of Ja'far; during this time Ja'far's wife had been unable to look after their hair. "The Prophet said, 'Do not weep over my brother after this day,' and he said, 'Call the children of my brother to me.' We were herded before him. He said, 'Call a barber.' He then ordered that our hair should be cut short."[87]

Concerning general appearance, the contemporary Islamic scholar Fethullah Gülen provides us with a clear understanding:

> As is reported in many books about the life of the Prophet, most Companions of God's Messenger had long, braided hair.

Some of them would gather it in a knot. In Bukhari's Al-Sahih, the following incident is narrated: Seeing a man who had knotted his hair during the Hajj, the Prophet advised him to untie his hair so that his hair, also, got the benefit from *sajda*, or prostration. God's Messenger did not order Abu Bakr, or Umar, or Uthman, all of whom had long hair, to cut their hair.

After the conquest of Mecca, the hearts of many people were softened and warmed towards Islam, and most of them embraced Islam. They wore garments in the style of nonbelievers and the turban of the unbelievers on their heads. The Prophet did not ask them to remove even these. Indeed, this would be formalism and he was far beyond formalism. He did not give any orders that could be interpreted as formalism.

In fact, outer appearance is not something essential in Islam, but rather, it is something of secondary importance. So, we should not be too concerned with outer appearance or formalism. The Prophet may have warned those who had cut some of their hair and left other parts, just as some young people do today, as it distorts the natural appearance and it would have been imitating non-Muslims. It is mentioned in the sections of hadith books that are concerned with garments and physical appearance, mainly in Tirmidhi, that the Prophet used to comb his hair according to the customs of the time in Mecca, so as not to resemble non-Muslims. After he emigrated to Medina and saw that Christians and Jews there combed their hair over their forehead (as in the historical pictures and films about Romans), he changed the way he combed his hair again and parted it in the middle and combed it to the right and to the left. Most likely, some people used to shave part of the head like the Christians and Jews. Therefore, the Prophet behaved in accordance with the hadith, "He who imitates a people is one of them."[88]

The human body is perfectly formed. It is formed with such subtle rules of geometry and mathematics that it is impossible not to appreciate its design. Therefore, it would probably not be correct to change something that has been created in such a perfect manner. In a hadith, the Prophet, peace and blessings be upon him, says, "God wants to see the signs of His blessings on His servants."[89] Therefore, it would not be incorrect to say that hair should be cut in a way that is suitable to its natural form.

But today, needless interference may have negative effects, even on devoted believers. Therefore, nobody should take the place of the Prophet and make negative comments on appearance, saying, "Cut your hair, tidy your clothes." This is not the way it should be said. If you say such things, those people will go away and never return to your world of thought.[90]

CHAPTER 3

What Good Character Requires

HILM (GENTLENESS)

H*ilm* means being inclined to gentleness or mildness; this adjective describes a person who is quiet and peaceful, slow to anger, quick to forgive, and who is in control of their lower nature. It also encompasses good *akhlaq* because it embodies behavior like patience and tolerance in the face of unpleasant situations, keeping one's cool when provoked, and remaining dignified, serious and calm in response to distressing or unkind treatment. *Hilm,* along with humility, is one of the characteristics that most pleases God. In fact, these two dispositions are the source and origin of all other good character traits.

In addition to dignity and calm, *hilm* also means to act with consciousness and without haste. The result is a good and moral manner which pleases God. *Hilm* is one of the basic elements of good morality. With *hilm* it is also possible to perfect the mind and to improve other aspects of one's temperament. Just as knowledge can be gained through learning, so *hilm* can be attained by making an effort. In other words, it is possible to reach *hilm* by working.

Hilm is also closely related to controlling one's negative responses and reactions. It is much more difficult for those who cannot control or reign their temper to attain a state of *hilm*. Scholars consider the ability to act with *hilm* to be among the most virtuous practices.

Humans are distinguished and privileged among all creatures. God Almighty blessed people with lofty attributes that He endowed on no other creature, like intelligence, conscience, mercy, compassion, empathy, and the desire to help, respect, and honor. For this reason, the human being is the most valuable being in all creation.

As we can see, *hilm* indicates total gentleness, as well as behavior such as overlooking faults, forgiving others, and being open to everyone for the sake of dialogue.

THE *HILM* (GENTLENESS) OF THE PROPHET

Our Prophet, both before and after his prophethood, was the gentlest of people. This is a quality that he carried throughout his life. God Himself protected the Prophet from ever losing his *hilm*, and was pleased with the Prophet because of it. God spoke of this in the Qur'an: "*It was by a mercy from God that (at the time of the setback), you (O Messenger) were lenient with your followers. Had you been harsh and hard-hearted, they would surely have scattered away from about you*" (Al Imran 3:159).

The Prophet never thought to avenge himself for wrongs done to his person. In addition, he was the hardest to anger, the easiest to please, and the most forgiving of all. When Prophet Muhammad, peace and blessings be upon him, began his prophetic mission to teach people about God's commands, the disbelievers in the Quraysh tribe leveled every kind of insult and indignity at him. They ridiculed the Prophet, threatened to kill him, spread thorns on his path, threw excrement at him, and even threw a noose around his neck and tried to drag him by it. Not stopping at this, they called him a conjurer and sorcerer, and said he was possessed; they tried everything they could think of to anger him. But the Prophet endured everything they did to him without reacting.

No one, whoever they may be, would be able to refrain from becoming angry, and thus react and try to respond in kind when insulted or attacked in such a way by others. Yet the Prophet did none of these things. He was extremely calm, patient, and tolerant. He strove to carry out the responsibility given to him by God. Perhaps this is why he did not respond to the torments he was subjected to.

Someone who heard the Prophet explaining Islam to people in the market place in Mecca related, "Muhammad, peace and blessings be upon him, was declaring the Oneness of God, and that those who believe in the One God would be saved. Abu Jahl started throwing rocks at him, and shouting, 'People, do not listen to this man! He is trying to get you to abandon your religion. He wants to separate you from our idols Lat and Uzza!' The Prophet refused to acknowledge the instigation; he did not once turn to look at Abu Jahl. He simply continued his duty."[1]

Another day, the Prophet was going to visit Sa'd ibn Ubada, one of the Companions who had fallen ill. On the way, he encountered a gathering assembled by the ringleader of the unbelievers, 'Abdullah ibn Ubayy. The Prophet stopped for a while. Ibn Ubayy began to taunt the Prophet, saying arrogantly, "Careful you, your animal is making dust. Get out of here, your animal is bothering us!" The Prophet greeted the group and then began to speak of Islam. Ibn Ubayy, seeing that the people were listening to him, was beside himself. Saying, "If anyone wants to hear something from you he will come to you! Do not talk to us of Islam!", he hurled curses at the Prophet. But the Prophet's *adab* would not let him respond in kind; he simply continued his address. On seeing this, the great poet 'Abdullah ibn Rawaha was moved; he stood up and said, "O Messenger of God, come here more often, and speak to us; we love you greatly!" Then a disagreement began between the Muslims and the disbelievers. They started to argue. The Prophet, calm and gentle as always, calmed them down and then departed, continuing on his way.[2]

The Jewish tribes living in the Arabian Peninsula at that time were among the Prophet's most relentless enemies. Some of them had a rancorous, jealous, greedy character. It should also be noted that these Jews took great pains to separate their own education, scholarship and literature from the Arabs, whom they believed to be inferior in these areas. As a result, they knew about the prophecies concerning the advent of a new Messenger, and were waiting for the coming of God's Messenger. When Prophet Muhammad, peace and blessings be upon him, first declared his prophetic mission from God, many Jews who had thought that the Prophet would be from the Children of Israel did not believe him. These enemies created the most evil strategies against him and tried desperately to get rid of him.

One of them cast a spell on the Prophet, who became ill and was confined to bed for several days. Finally Archangel Gabriel came and told him, "O Muhammad, one from among the Jewish people cast a spell on you by throwing a knotted string into (such and such a well). Send someone there and have him remove the string." The Prophet sent Ali, who took out the knotted string and brought it to him. As soon as they untied the knot he was released from the illness and got well. Although he knew who had done this, the Prophet never confronted the perpetrator about it.[3]

However, there were, of course, good and righteous people among the People of the Book (those who had been blessed with previous Revelations; that is, the Jews and Christians); there were those who sought the truth. There were many signs and much knowledge in the earlier Scriptures regarding the unique characteristics and virtues of the coming Prophet, that is, Prophet Muhammad, peace and blessings be upon him.

One of the most easily recognizable of the signs related in the Torah about the coming Prophet was his *hilm*. The Torah proclaimed that the Prophet would be of gentle spirit and show great patience and tolerance in inviting the people to God's way. The Jewish scholars saw with their own eyes that the Prophet had many qualities which the Torah had predicted. Some of them continued to search and question, and when they saw all of the signs fulfilled in the Prophet they believed him.

One of these Jewish scholars, thinking, "I have seen in him every single sign and characteristic foretold in the Torah except *hilm*," decided to test this last trait. "I went and lent the Prophet thirty *dinar* for a specified time. Then I went to him one day before the payment date and said, 'O Muhammad, pay me back. You sons of Abdul Muttalib never pay your debts on time.'" Hearing this, Umar retorted, "O foul Jew, by God, if we were not in the Messenger's house, I would slap your face." But the Messenger said to Umar, "O Umar, God forgive you. I expected better from you. You should have said that I would gladly pay what I owe him, and you should have said that you would assist him to collect it and acted courteously toward him."

The Jewish man recounts, "The Messenger responded to my ignorant, harsh, rude manner only by increasing his own gentleness. He said to me, 'O Jewish man, I will surely pay you back tomorrow morning.' Then he told Umar, 'O Umar, tomorrow morning take him to whichever date grove he wishes, and give him as much as he wishes. Then give him more than he asks for. If he is not pleased with the dates in that grove, take him to another one.'

"The following day Umar brought me to the date grove of my choice. He gave me as much as the Messenger had told him to, and added even more." The Jewish man, after being repaid in this manner by the Prophet, declared the *shahada*, or testimony of faith, and became a Muslim. He explained his conversion to Umar as follows: "O Umar, do you know why I acted that way to the Messenger of God? I acted thus because I saw in him all of the characteristics and morals foretold in the writings of the Torah. The only ones I had not observed were *hilm* and kindness. Today I tried his patience, and he responded just as the Torah said he would. With you as my witness, I hereby donate these dates and half of all my possessions to the poor among the Muslims." This one simple demonstration of the Prophet's patience and gentleness brought many other people to belief.[4]

The Prophet responded to words and actions that were turned against him with maturity, compassion, and kindness. He exhibited *akhlaq* to a level that others could never possibly reach. Abu Said al-Khudri narrates, "The Prophet was distributing the spoils from the Battle of Hunayn to the Companions who had fought.

He gave a bit more from the captured property to some of the Companions. Among them were Aqra ibn Habis and Uyayna ibn Hisn, who each received a hundred camels. When this happened Dhu al-Khuwaysira of the house of Tamim came to him and objected, saying, 'O Messenger of God! Do not swerve from equality and justice. By God, this distribution cannot be pleasing to God!' The Prophet was saddened and answered, 'Shame on you, if I do not act justly, who will? For if I do not carry out justice, I will earn a terrible punishment. May God's mercy be on Moses, he was patient in the face of worse insults than this.'"[5]

Another time the Prophet was in the mosque with the Companions, sitting and talking with them. A Bedouin entered and prayed two *rakat*s of *salat*, then opened his hands and prayed, "O God, have mercy on me and on Muhammad. Do not have mercy on anyone else." When the Prophet heard him praying thus, he said, "You are limiting God's great and wide mercy," thus correcting the Bedouin's mistake.

A little later, the Bedouin got up, went to a corner of the mosque, and urinated there. When the Companions saw what he was doing they jumped up to stop him. The Prophet, however, intervened and told them, "Leave him alone. Let him see what he has done. Later, go and wash it with a bucket of water, for you have been sent to make the way easier, not to complicate." Then he called the Bedouin to his side and told him, "Mosques are not for relieving ourselves or for any other kind of uncleanness. They are made for the remembrance of God, praying, and reading the Qur'an."[6]

This incident happened in the mosque that our Prophet had helped build with his own hands for the purpose of worship; the man had made a very great error. But the Prophet knew that the Bedouin had not done so intentionally, but rather out of ignorance.

It is only when one is confronted with repulsive behavior that a display of understanding, tolerance and gentleness can be truly meaningful; it is at such times that being forgiving and forbearing are most difficult. Indeed, anyone can be patient and calm during normal situations. Just as he was in every other way, the Prophet was extraordinary in his *hilm* and gentleness. In fact he was utterly unique; it would be impossible to find his equal.

Anas ibn Malik tells of another example of the *hilm* and gentleness of the Prophet: "I was walking with the Prophet. He was wearing a garment made of rough Najran fabric. A Bedouin came running up behind the Prophet, grabbed his robe and yanked it back. His garment was torn and his neck rubbed raw by this roughness." The man had yanked it so hard and the fabric was so rough that it left an angry welt on the Prophet's neck. Then the man said, "O Muhammad! Load my camels with grain. For the possessions you hold do not belong to you nor to your father."

The Bedouin's behavior was rude and uncouth, and the Prophet was troubled. He turned to the man and said, "First apologize, for you have injured me." The Bedouin retorted, "No, I will not apologize." The Prophet was trying to guide him in the way of courtesy, but the other man was unconcerned. The Prophet then turned to the Companions and, ignoring the man's incivility, instructed them, "Load one of this man's camels with barley, and the other with dates." The man, satisfied, went away. The Companions were surprised by the Prophet's kind treatment of this rude Bedouin.[7]

Likewise, our Prophet treated all those under his authority and in his service with the utmost gentleness; he did not get angry with them or hurt their feelings. Even if they were negligent in their duties or did not do what they said they would, he would only inquire with kindness and polite consideration.

Anas ibn Malik, who was in his service for many years, spoke of the *akhlaq* of the Prophet: "I served the Messenger for ten years. He never once showed impatience with me, never reproved me for neglecting to do something, nor ever asked me why I had done something I was not supposed to do."[8]

Anas recalled one time when the Prophet had to admonish him for neglecting his duty, "The Messenger of God sent me out one day with a task. At first I said, 'By God, I cannot go.' But inwardly I felt compelled to go wherever he sent me. I went out, and then I came across some children playing on the street. I forgot myself and started playing with them. Then the Prophet came up behind me, and put his hand on my head. I looked at his face, and he was smiling. 'Dear Anas, did you go where I sent you?' he asked. 'Yes, I am going, O Messenger of God,' I said."[9]

The Prophet's wife Aisha said that the Prophet once advised her, "O Aisha, be gentle. For wherever gentleness is found, its presence beautifies, but wherever gentleness is absent, its absence is ugly."[10]

Our Prophet's true courage and heroism was not in the physical strength to overpower, but in the knowledge and ability to stay calm when something upset him and to act gently even when he was offended.

'Abdullah ibn Mas'ud relates, "The Messenger of God said, 'Who among you do you call a hero?' We answered, 'One whom the wrestlers cannot defeat; one who cannot be overcome.' He replied, 'No, that is not a hero. The hero is one who can control himself when offended, the one who always practices self-mastery and temperance.'"[11]

From this perspective, Prophet Muhammad, peace and blessings be upon him, was a hero in the true sense of the word. He could not be defeated by his enemies in this aspect as well; those who sought to defeat his self-control, to overwhelm his restraint, could not do so. Instead, God's Messenger responded to wrongs done against his person with forbearance.

According to a narration of Jarir ibn 'Abdullah, the Prophet said, "Without a doubt, God rewards gentleness and kindness, not harshness and roughness. And when God loves one of His servants, He grants them the blessing of gentleness. A person or household bereft of this blessing is bereft of everything."[12]

The "gentleness and kindness" referred to here means a mature morality which requires, on principle, that one never loses one's temper. To get irritated and fly into a rage at any time is totally contrary to the nature of *hilm,* which entails a gentle and morally upright character. Thus, disciplining oneself in this one area—by cooling a quick temper and avoiding irritability—can bring a great number of positive effects and make great changes in one's morality.

Abdur Rahman ibn Awf relates, "Once someone came to our Prophet and asked, 'O Messenger of God! Teach me words with which I can attain comfort and peace. But let them be brief, so I won't forget.' The Prophet replied, 'Don't lose your temper!'"[13]

Our Beloved Prophet taught us that there is also a satanic side to anger, and gave a practical solution: "Anger is from Satan, and Satan is created from fire. Fire can only be put out with water. For this reason, when you become angry, make ablutions."[14] Another helpful solution from the Prophet is, "When one of you becomes angry, if he is standing, let him immediately sit down. If his anger passes, good; if it does not, let him lie down."[15]

DEFUSING HATRED AND ANIMOSITY

Harboring rancor and animosity means looking for revenge and retribution. The heart of one who is envious or rapacious has been darkened and their mental facilities are taken over by vengeance. This feeling of vengeance grows until it pushes out all the love and faith in a person, and they begin to put revenge before everything, even obedience to God.

By contrast, freeing the heart of rancor and enmity quickly brings a psychological balance and harmony between the heart and mind, the physical and the spiritual. A person who can keep their temper under control will be of greater benefit to society and able to cultivate their higher emotions to their full potential.

In the Qur'an God tells us that the rancor and enmity harbored by people have a dangerous potential to trigger injustice:

> O you who believe! Be upholders and standard-bearers of right for God's sake, being witnesses for (the establishment of) absolute justice. And by no means let your detestation for a people (or their detestation for you) move you to (commit the sin of) deviating from justice. Be just: this is nearer and more suited to righteousness and piety. Seek righteousness and piety and always act in reverence for God. Surely God is fully aware of all that you do. (Maeda 5:8)

Every type of anger and vexation gives rise to mental problems and physical illnesses. Without sincere forgiveness, without "letting go," total recovery is impossible. Hatred, animosity, rage, wanting to "get even" or see others punished, even criticism and reproach, all pollute the mind, weaken the soul, and eventually ruin a person's health. It could be said that overcoming anger can be achieved if one nurtures a desire to help others and trains one's thoughts along these lines, as well as trying to seek to live a life that is more "behind the scenes" rather than striving to be the center of attention. In the Qur'an God says,

> They spend (out of what God has provided for them,) both in ease and hardship, ever-restraining their rage (even when provoked and able to retaliate), and pardoning people (their offenses). God loves (such) people who are devoted to doing good, aware that God is seeing them. (Al Imran 3:134)

Human nature is created in such a way that a person can fluctuate between good and bad. Knowing this, it is necessary to know how to deal with one's own ego, keeping in mind that good comes from God while evil comes from the ego and leads to ultimate destruction. A person who knows that they are prone to vacillating between good and bad actions must expend extra energy to ensure that they refrain from major sins and to avoid situations that could lead to doing wrong: *"Those who avoid the major sins and indecent, shameful deeds (which are indeed to be counted among major sins), and when they become angry, even then they forgive (rather than retaliate in kind)"* (Shura 42:37).

Furthermore, in order to avoid anger or antipathy, we have been given several strong mainstays, such as praying for one's own forgiveness, the forgiveness of our brothers and sisters in religion, and that of our spiritual ancestors, asking God not to allow seeds of bitterness and anger against believing people grow in our hearts, and expecting these prayers to be accepted; these are all stated in the following Qur'anic verse:

> And all those who come after them (and follow in their footsteps) pray, "O our Lord! Forgive us and our brothers (and sisters) in Religion who have preceded us in faith, and let not our hearts entertain any ill-feeling against any of the believers. O our Lord! You are All-Forgiving, All-Compassionate (especially toward Your believing servants). (Hashr 59:10)

There are also some useful indications in the life and practice of Prophet Muhammad, peace and blessings be upon him, regarding the control of anger and animosity. Some of these enlightening hadith are as follows.

The Prophet warned Anas ibn Malik while the latter was still a child, telling Anas that he should forgive those who had done him wrong, and thus avoid having his spirit sullied with enmity or lingering resentment. Anas ibn Malik related the following narration from the Messenger of God: "My child! Every morning and every evening, make sure you hold no grudge or enmity against anyone. Do this, if you can, my child! This is my example. Whoever follows my example truly loves me. And whoever loves me will be with me in Paradise."[16] As we can see, those who can purify their hearts of jealousy, anger, and animosity will be together with the Prophet and reach Heaven.

Anger that burns the soul brings a feeling of vengefulness to the heart and can feed vengeful actions. Some people easily lose their temper. They are merciless, severe, and cruel. Some people, though they have quick tempers, are also quick to recover from anger.

In this regard the Prophet divided people into three basic groups, according to how quickly they anger and how quickly their anger departs. He also explained which one of these groups is most virtuous. In addition, he gives an immediate practical solution for anger: taking ablutions to help the feeling subside.

Abu Said al-Khudri narrated, "God's Messenger said, 'Be aware that there are people who are slow to anger and quick to repent of their anger; there are also people who are quick to anger and quick to get over it. There is also a third group of people, who anger quickly and are slow to let their anger go. The best of these are those who are slow to anger and quick to turn from anger. The worst are those who are quick to anger and are slow to let their anger go. Beware! Anger is like a burning ember in the heart of man. Do you not see the eyes that glow and the cheeks that puff out? Whoever feels himself beginning to get angry, he should touch the ground...."[17]

Accordingly, taking ablutions or bathing as well as touching the ground or walking on the soil barefoot are some practical ways of dispelling anger. But there is another dimension as well: one who feels overwhelmed by anger should seek refuge in God.

Muadh ibn Jabal relates, "Two people cursed each other in the presence of the Messenger. The face of one of them showed anger at the other. God's Messenger said, 'I know a word that you can say to ward off the anger that I see in your face. That is *a'udhu billahi min ash-shaytan ar-rajim* (I seek refuge in God from Satan, who is eternally rejected from God's Mercy).'"[18]

Abu Hurayra provided the following hadith: "A man asked the Prophet, 'O Messenger of God! Give me a short, easy piece of advice, that I won't forget it.' He repeated his request several times, and the Prophet answered with, 'Don't get angry!'"[19]

A person with a quick temper should be careful not to miss good advice or exhortation by becoming upset at being urged to that which is good or commendable (and therefore not listening to the other person). Ibn Abbas narrates that when Uyayna ibn Hisn came to Medina, he stayed with his nephew Hurr ibn Qays, who was a person whom Umar used to keep near him as one of the learned men who knew the Qur'an by heart (*qurra*) and who by virtue of their knowledge can give legal opinion or judgment (*fuqaha*). Uyayna said to his nephew, "O nephew! You are close to this ruler, so ask him for an audience for me!" So the nephew asked Caliph Umar for this. But when Ibn Hisn came into Umar's presence, he said, "Beware! O the son of Khattab! By God, you neither give us enough provision nor judge among us with justice!" Umar was extremely upset. He was almost ready to hit Uyayna when Hurr jumped up and said,

"O Ruler of the Believers, God said to His Messenger, '*Adopt the way of forbearance and tolerance, and enjoin what is good and right, and withdraw from the ignorant ones (do not care what they say and do)*' (A'raf 7:199). This man is ignorant." When Hurr recited this verse Umar instantly froze in his tracks; he could not ignore the Qur'an, so he did nothing to the insolent man.[20]

A person who is overwhelmed by anger will have trouble making sound decisions. There is a direct prohibition regarding situations like this. Abu Bakr told his son 'Abdullah, who was serving as a judge, "When you are angry, do not judge between two people. For the Messenger said, 'No one should judge between others when he is angry.'"[21]

Concerning the verse, "*Goodness and evil can never be equal. Repel evil with what is better (or best). Then see: the one between whom and you there was enmity has become a bosom friend. And none are ever enabled to attain it (such great virtue) save those who are patient (in adversities and against the temptations of their souls and Satan), and none are ever enabled to attain it save those who have a great part in human perfections and virtues*" (Fussilat 41:34–35), Ibn Abbas said, "'*what is better (or best)*' in this verse means 'patience at the moment of anger, and forgiveness at the moment we are wronged.' If people do these things, God will protect them from their enemies; He will cause their enemies to become friends for them."[22]

RETURNING EVIL WITH GOOD

Wickedness is weak, even when it seems to be victorious. In fact wickedness cannot escape the destiny of its ultimate destruction. Goodness, honesty, and righteousness are the conquerors of the heart, and they are powerful in and of themselves. When good and evil truly come head to head with one another, there are very few people who will not respect good and despise evil. This clearly demonstrates that goodness and evil cannot be one.

It is goodness to forgive a wrong. But to return evil with good on top of forgiveness is to win over the heart of the one who was against you.

> And none are ever enabled to attain it (such great virtue) save those who are patient (in adversities and against the temptations of their souls and Satan), and none are ever enabled to attain it save those who have a great part in human perfections and virtues. And if a prompting from Satan should stir in you (when carrying out your mission or during worship or in your daily life), seek refuge in God immediately. He is the One Who is the All-Hearing, the All-Knowing. (Fussilat 41:35–36)

In terms of the struggle between good and evil, Satan is grievously disappointed when believers respond to evil with good. For he wants the believers to do something wrong, even some small reaction, so that he can use it to create doubts in the believers. In fact, if the believers show even the tiniest bit of excess in their response to those who attack them, some might say that "they were influenced by Satan's whispers." This will cause the believers to lose a large part of their power. By reacting they cast a small shadow over their righteousness, even if they were completely in the right, and those who see this shadow will have, to some extent, an excuse. The following hadith provides a very useful commentary on the verse above:

One day a man came up to Abu Bakr and began to heap insults on him. The Prophet, peace and blessings be upon him, was also there. As the man insulted him, Abu Bakr listened but gave no reply. The Prophet was smiling. Finally Abu Bakr could no longer stand it and gave a harsh retort. The Prophet's countenance changed and he left. Abu Bakr followed him out to ask him why he left. He answered, "When you were quiet, there was an angel answering on your behalf. But when you opened your mouth, Satan showed up. I cannot stay in the same place as Satan."[23]

In relation to this issue of repelling falsehood with truth and responding with what is the best in conduct, the Qur'an says,

> (But whatever they may say or do,) repel the evil (done to you and committed against your mission) with the best (of what you can do). We know best all that they falsely attribute to Us. And say, "My Lord! I seek refuge in You from the promptings and provocations of the satans (of the jinn and humankind especially in my relations with people, while I am performing my mission). I seek refuge in You, my Lord, lest they be present with me." (Mu'minun 23:96–98)

Just as one must refuse to heed slights and wrongs, it is also important to respond to wrongs with the best possible positive action.

> Adopt the way of forbearance and tolerance, and enjoin what is good and right, and withdraw from the ignorant ones (do not care what they say and do). And if a prompting from Satan should cause you hurt (as you carry out your mission or during worship or in your everyday life), seek refuge in God. He is All-Hearing, All-Knowing. (A'raf 7:199–200)

A believer is commanded to take refuge in God when they hear any whispers from within themselves that urge them to take an action that is against God's commands and which will not please God. In every situation when a person is subject to such whispers regarding the essentials of faith, worship, prohibitions, or how to treat people— in short, any aspect of life—they must turn to God and seek His protection. On the surface, the verse above seems to be addressed to the Prophet, but it is in fact intended for all people.

> Those who keep from disobedience to God in reverence for Him and piety: when a suggestion from Satan touches them— they are alert and remember God, and then they have clear discernment. Whereas their brothers (the brothers of the satans in the form of human beings)—satans draw them deeper into error and do not relax in their efforts. (A'raf 7:201–202)

Those who refrain from setting themselves against God never feel completely secure that they will do no wrong. Satan also tries to influence them. He can cloud their vision and they are potentially susceptible to the images and ideas he puts in their heads. But before long they will perceive the truth, remembering that they must seek refuge in God; their understanding will become clear and thus they will be saved from doing wrong.

Consider the promise of reward announced by our Prophet for the person who avoids an argument, even if they are in the right: "For the person who avoids an argument, even when they are in the right, I guarantee a mansion in the corner of Heaven. And for the one who never lies, even in jest, there is a mansion in the center of Heaven. And for the person of good morals, I guarantee a mansion at the highest level of Heaven."[24]

MODESTY, SHYNESS, AND FEELING
ASHAMED OF WRONG ACTS

H*aya*, an instinctive feeling of shame combined with the modesty based on Islam, forms the greatest safeguard against shameful or indecent behavior.

Prophet Muhammad, peace and blessings be upon him, said, "Every religion has a moral code. And the moral code of Islam is *haya*," thereby emphasizing the importance of this feeling in the life of a Muslim. The following hadith also explains this crucial characteristic. 'Abdullah ibn Umar reported that the Prophet came upon a man who advised his brother not to be too shy. The Prophet said, "Stop; *haya* comes from faith." Another hadith says, "Faith has seventy rays. The highest degree is to say *La ilaha illallah*, ("There is no deity other than God") and the least degree is to remove something harmful from the road. And *haya* is one portion of faith."[25] This hadith was explained by Ibn al-Athir thus:

"Despite the fact that it is an inborn natural feeling, *haya* can also be gained and developed with practice. *Haya* keeps one away from sins; it comes between a person and their sins. This means it has a function in a person's faith. The hadith mentions that it is 'one portion of faith.' Faith includes the action of following God's commands and avoiding that which He has forbidden. Thus, when *haya* causes a person to avoid sins, it becomes like a portion of faith."[26]

Haya demands awareness of God's Presence and thus the practicing of self-control or self-supervision. According to a narration of Ibn Mas'ud, the Prophet said, "Be fully conscious of God, as God requires you to be." When someone asked, "O God's Messenger! How does God require us to be conscious?" He answered, "Whoever protects his head and what is in it, his stomach and the organs attached to it, whoever is not attracted to the ornaments of the world, and does not forget that death and decay follow has the *haya* that God requires."[27]

To "protect the head" in this sense means to use the brain and its power to think in positive ways. The other organs should also be "protected" by avoiding forbidden things, not eating prohibited foods, and not telling lies or using unpleasant words. The "organs connected to the stomach" are the sex organs, which must be protected by avoiding extramarital sexual contact. Thinking more broadly, hands and feet can also be seen as being "connected to the stomach." So it can be said that the hadith teaches us to keep the hands, arms, feet, and so on from committing sins. This is the meaning of "shyness," or *haya*, in the sense God requires.

The feeling originating from faith which we refer to here must be distinguished from other characteristics that make a person timid, passive, or unwilling to step forward to fulfill their responsibilities. For example, it is not good for women to hang back out of "shyness" when it comes to education. If they do not have the opportunity to learn from other women, they should not hesitate to ask a man who is considered knowledgeable in religious matters or in other areas. Indeed, if there is a religious question they need to know and they do not ask a man out of "shyness," it will cause them to fail to accomplish their religious duties correctly.

Our Prophet personally answered the particular questions of women, and also had his wife Aisha teach them in his place. Aisha had these notable words to say about women who showed no shame in seeking religious knowledge: "What good women the Ansar women were. Their bashfulness did not prevent them from learning their religion well."[28]

One who wishes to be granted felicity in this world and the next must strive to have *adab* and *haya*. A person who has a sense of *haya* fears to do wrong not only where other people can see them, but also when they are alone. Such a person has a healthy spirit and a peaceful conscience. We can recognize them by their geniality, their humility, and their trustworthiness.

Qurra ibn Iyas said, "We were together with the Prophet. Someone spoke of *haya*: 'O God's Messenger, is *haya* part of religion?' they asked. The Prophet's answer was, '*Haya* is the completion of religion. Without a doubt *haya*, curbing the tongue, and chastity all arise from faith. These increase a person's rewards in the next life, and lessen desire for the things of this world. But that which is given in the next life is greater than that which is lessened in this world.'"[29]

A person with *haya* does not have faults like lying, cheating, being dishonest, stealing, bribing others, holding a grudge, or slandering others. When someone loses the veil of *haya*, they no longer fear the wrath of God or feel shame about such things as stealing from the poor; such a person would not even be moved by the tears of the victims of hunger or disaster.

Haya indicates the strength of a person's faith and their level of *adab*. *Haya* is the foundation of goodness and the basic element of every type of good. It is a barricade against sins that can destroy the heart. God Almighty says in the Qur'an,

> Say, "My Lord has made unlawful only indecent, shameful deeds (like fornication, adultery, prostitution, and homosexuality), whether those of them that are apparent and committed openly or those that are committed secretly; and any act explicitly sinful; and insolence and offenses (against the Religion, life, personal property, others' chastity, and mental and bodily health), which is openly unjustified; and (it is also forbidden) that you associate partners with God for which He has sent no authority at all, and that you speak against God the things about which you have no sure knowledge. (A'raf 7:33)

In short, a Muslim should be extremely cautious in thoughts and acts, always guarding their tongue from speaking wrongly, their eyes from looking at that which is prohibited, their ears from listening to the private conversations of others, and all their limbs from committing wrong acts.

TRUTHFULNESS

Honesty and being straightforward are characteristics that are manifested both in thought and deed. The honesty of a true believer can never be compromised. The Qur'an very clearly declares the greatness of honesty and integrity. God's Word says, *"O you who believe! Act in reverence for God and piously, without doing anything to incur His punishment, and always speak words true, proper and straight to the point"* (Ahzab 33:70). This verse tells us that a person of faith must always be honest; even when we have done something wrong, we must never lie to cover it up. Instead, whenever we make a mistake, we should immediately apologize and try to compensate for the wrong.

A person who has internalized the fundamental moral quality of honesty would never lie, not for any reason whatsoever; they never see telling an untruth as an option or a solution. Therefore, a person who practices the morality taught in the Qur'an does not have to bear the burden and consequences of lying.

Those who say, *"Our Lord is God"* (Fussilat 41:30), and steadfastly pursue the right way, according to this verse, will be visited by angels who say, *"Do not fear or grieve; but rejoice in the glad tidings of Paradise which you have been promised)"* (Fussilat 41:30). People with integrity and sincerity will live a peaceful life, as they can be trusted.

Moreover, one who adopts this admirable way of life while in the world will experience even better rewards in the next life. God has promised such rewards to those who are righteous and honest:

> God will say, "This is the Day when their truthfulness (faithfulness and steadfastness) will benefit all who were true to their word (to God). For them are Gardens through which rivers flow, therein to abide for ever. God is well-pleased with them,

and they are well-pleased with Him. That is the supreme triumph." (Maeda 5:119)

The essence of being righteous is to "*Pursue what is exactly right (in every matter of the Religion) as you are commanded (by God)...*" (Hud 11:112; Shura 42:15). God sent the Prophets as examples of righteousness and integrity. Prophet Muhammad, peace and blessings be upon him, and all the Prophets sent before him were the quintessence of righteousness. The Qur'an also mentions righteousness and truthfulness when describing the qualities of Abraham, Ishmael, and Enoch, peace be upon them all (Maryam 19:41, 54, 56).

Prophet Muhammad, peace and blessings be upon him, also taught about honesty in some hadith. Ibn Mas'ud explains, "God's Messenger said, 'Loyalty and truthfulness will lead a person to do good things that please God, and these in turn will bring that person to Paradise. For he will speak honestly and seek after righteousness and in the end will be recorded as eminently truthful in the presence of God. But lies will lead a person to overstep the bounds, and this in turn will bring him to the Fire. A lying person will pursue lies and in the end he will be recorded as a great liar in the presence of God.'"[30]

In another hadith from Abu Musa, the Prophet spoke of the reward of a truthful Muslim who is worthy of being charged with protecting someone else's property: "The faithful trustee who gives what he is commanded completely and in full with a good will (takes good care of what is entrusted to him), and who delivers it to the one whom he was told to give it, is regarded as one of the two (i.e., God gives him reward like the owner of the trust) for giving charity." In a different version of the same hadith, Nasai adds, "A believer is like a wall for another believer; they can lean on and rely upon one another."[31]

HONESTY IN SPEECH

An important fundamental of Islamic morality is truthfulness and making every effort toward achieving transparency (this applies to business and personal relations on every level).

The Messenger of God showed great care to ensure that children acquired the ethic of always speaking the truth. In order to prevent parents from making the mistake of lying to their children or perpetrating any such type of dishonesty with them, the Prophet taught general principles that guide the parent–child relationship. For instance, he said it is unacceptable to mislead or deceive children under any circumstances, and warned parents against any type of carelessness in their relationship with their children. There is an interesting hadith about this. 'Abdullah ibn Amr recalls, "One day my mother called me. God's Messenger was sitting in our house. My mother told me, 'Come here and I'll give you something.' God's Messenger asked her, 'What are you going to give him?' She answered, 'I'm going to give him a date.' So the Prophet said, 'Be warned, if you had not been planning to give him something, it would have been written in your book of deeds as a lie, a sin.'"[32] Abu Hurayra also relates a similar narration: "God's Messenger said, 'Whoever says to a child, "Come here, I will give you something," and then does not give them anything will be accountable for lying.'"[33]

HONESTY OF CHARACTER

A Muslim's inner conformity to his or her outer appearance is also critical for integrity. Just as we are to refrain from harmful words, so too must we restrain ourselves from hateful feelings or thoughts. In other words, a Muslim should speak as they think, and act according to their word; there should be no difference between who they are inside and who they appear to be. The following hadith addresses this aspect of integrity: "A person whose heart is not correct cannot have correct faith. If the tongue does not speak truth, the heart cannot be right, and if the person's neighbors are not safe from him, he cannot enter Paradise."[34] Here the Prophet teaches that the heart and the tongue should be consistent with each other, and both of them should manifest integrity.

Honesty in Business

When there is consistency between a Muslim's inner self and outer actions, they will always be honest, both at work and in business. A Muslim must be careful never to cheat or deceive others to gain greater profit or for any other reason.

A hadith handed down by Abu Hurayra reports, "One day the Prophet saw (a man selling) a heap of wheat. He put his hand into the pile and found that, while the top was dry, the bottom was damp. He asked the seller, 'What is this?' The man said, 'The rain wet it.' The Prophet responded, 'You should put the wet part on top (so people can see it). One who cheats us is not of us.'"[35]

One of the most unique characteristics of the blessed Companions of the Prophet—perhaps their most important characteristic—was their unfailing integrity and righteousness. These qualities brought a deep atmosphere of peace and security to their inner lives as well as to their interpersonal relations.

Once Abu al-Hawra asked Hasan ibn Ali ibn Abu Talib, "What have you memorized from God's Messenger?" He answered, "Turn away from whatever gives you doubts or misgivings, and look at that which does not! For righteousness gives the heart rest, but lies bring uncertainty and suspicion."[36] In a similar narration, Sufyan ibn 'Abdullah al-Sakafi said, "O Messenger of God, give me such knowledge of Islam that it will suffice me and I will never need to ask anyone else about Islam." He answered, "Say, 'I believe in God,' and then be completely honest in everything."[37]

HUMOR AND JOKES

When kidding and joking with friends, the thing to pay the most attention to is not to say something that is untrue. Unfortunately, the majority of people actually "lie" when they joke. There is a good quotation from our Prophet, peace and blessings be upon him, about this: Abu Hurayra tells how some of the Companions said to the Prophet, "'O Messenger, you are kidding us!" He said, "Certainly, even if it is a joke, I always speak the truth!"[38]

Jokes that are not based on untruths are good for relaxing the mind. We should also be careful not to be hurtful while making jokes. For instance, it is one thing to make pleasant jokes appropriate to a child's age, but it is quite another to make jokes at their expense or to belittle them. Whether a person is mature or still a child, giving them the feeling that you are laughing at something they think important is very destructive. In particular, a joke that intends to belittle another person always has a cruel side.

Many people think that any kind of joke is acceptable as long as they or others are having a good time. But looking closer, there may be ulterior motives at work, particularly if what is said gives one the "upper hand" or some kind of power over the other person. Such motives may arise from an impulse to mock or relish another person's difficulties, or to belittle them. Or it may be an attempt to make others think that we are clever; we may see mockery as humorous or perhaps we just do not accept responsibility for what we say and do. But it is common sense that no one likes to be the butt of a joke, even if it is perpetrated by their best friend. The Prophet instructed, "Let none of you take his brother's (another person's) property, in jest or for any other reason. If anyone takes (even) the staff of his brother, he should return it."[39]

There is no need to point out that such aggressive "kidding" is much more than a simple joke. Similarly, it is not acceptable to try to scare people for fun. For example, putting on a frightening mask to scare people and laugh at their fear is not moral behavior. In fact, the Prophet forbade children and adults to play scary tricks on one another. Ibn Abi Layla says, "The Prophet's Companions told us that once while they were on a journey, someone took another person's rope while he was sleeping. When he woke up, the man was afraid he had lost it. When the Prophet saw this, he said, 'It is not permissible for a Muslim to frighten another Muslim!'"[40]

It is cruel beyond words to frighten a little child whose motor skills and mental development have not yet matured. They will only feel angry, belittled, and confused at such "jokes." Parents and close relatives of the child in particular should take care that they never do such things. On the contrary, they should give the child reason to trust them as they play a key role in the child's ability to develop trust. Therefore, joking about a child's imperfections or clumsiness is absolutely repugnant and should not be permitted. Such actions can harm children irrevocably and negatively affect their capacity to develop social skills.

TEASING AND MOCKING

The Qur'an commands that people should not make fun of, embarrass, or ridicule one another, nor call each other by unbecoming nicknames. This is an important principle if there are to be good relations among people in a community.

> O you who believe! Let not some people among you deride another people, it may be that the latter are better than the former; nor let some women deride other women, it may be that the latter are better than the former. Nor defame one another (and provoke the same for yourselves in retaliation), nor insult one another with nicknames (that your brothers and sisters dislike). Evil is using names with vile meaning after (those so addressed have accepted) the faith (– doing so is like replacing a mark of faith with a mark of transgression). Whoever (does that and then) does not turn to God in repentance, (giving up doing so), those are indeed wrongdoers. (Hujurat 49:11)

Here I will address the issues in this verse, using Elmalili Hamdi Yazir as a source, but attempting to simplify his ideas. After the verse opens with a call to believers to conscientiously treat each other well, it inspires believers to do so with the greatest sincerity, indicating that this will make it possible for many more nations and people to perceive and accept the beauty of Islam. Then, this verse goes on from generally fostering brotherhood to teaching people the *adab* of how to treat each other, both face to face and when apart. There were several events that occasioned the revelation of this verse:

1. According to a narration from Dahhaq, several people from the tribe of Banu Tamim teased and mocked Companions

like Bilal al-Habashi, Habbab, Ammar, Suhayb, Abu Dharr, Salim, and Mawla Hudayfa.

2. Aisha said she used to tease Zaynab bint Huzayma al-Hila-liyya for being short. Likewise she and Hafsa talked between themselves about how short Umm Salama was.

3. Ibn Abbas relates that Safiyya bint Huyayy once came to the Messenger and said, "The women call me 'Jew, daughter of a Jew' to tease me." The Messenger replied, "Why do you not reply, 'My father was Aaron, my uncle was Moses, and my husband is Muhammad'?"

4. Thabit ibn Qays was partially deaf and therefore when he was near the Prophet, other people would let him through the crowd so he could come closer to hear. One day he came and started going through the others, saying, "Move, make room." One man did not pay attention, and Thabit became offended and asked, "Who is this?" The man told him his name. The other retorted, "No, you are the son of the woman who—" attributing him to a woman known for indecency. The man was embarrassed, and when this verse was revealed, Thabit never talked about nobleness by birth again.

5. Ikrima, the son of Abu Jahl (Islam's most determined enemy), became Muslim, but he was called "Son of the Pharaoh of the community of believers." This upset him and he told the Prophet about it.[41]

According to Qurtubi, to mock someone means that one is looking down on them, insulting them, putting them down, and talking about their faults in order to ridicule them. Razi says from a community point of view, mocking another person means "showing one's believing brother or sister less than their deserved respect and honor, approaching them in an uncomplimentary way." In the above verse the words *qawm* (tribe) and *nisa* (women) are used, which in Arabic denotes the men and the women of the community. There are other linguistic clues as well which prove this. The concept of the community is important in this verse in several ways:

1. It serves as a reminder that Islam is not a religion solely for private practice, but is meant to be lived as a community.
2. It shows that mocking others can cause serious problems and individuals must cease to practice such behavior.
3. The verse also implies that this action or habit on the part of one individual becomes like a sickness that affects the whole community, as a person who mocks others will always have some hangers-on laughing at the jokes and trying to become their friend by doing the same. If any question remains as to why such actions are forbidden, every believer should be concerned about the final reason: It may be that, in God's sight, the one who is mocked is actually better than the one who is mocking. For we can only know the outer appearance of others; God alone knows their hearts. We are not capable of knowing what level of value a person has in front of God. Therefore, no one has the right to belittle, look down on, or make fun of another person because of some outward appearance or action; this may be misleading. If the person we mock is greatly loved by God and we show them disrespect, then surely we will have wronged our own soul as well as that of the person. In other words, making fun of others is wrong in two ways: First, if a Muslim mocks another believer, they are mocking themselves, since we are all like one body. Second, if a person does something shameful, it brings shame most of all on their own soul. Thus, the verse can be paraphrased like this: "Do not mock, embarrass, or belittle believers; for to do so is to mock, embarrass, and belittle yourself." Or, if we look at it from the second aspect, "When you make a fool of someone or demean them, the result is that you have made a fool of yourself and besmirched your own name." In other words, the first mean-

ing is more to do with brotherhood, while the second meaning pertains to the honor and dignity of our individual soul.

A nickname is given either to honor someone or to bring them down in some way. The verse uses the word *nabz* to refer to epithets with derogatory meanings; these are forbidden. On the other hand, it is permissible to give or use positive epithets. According to Kashshaf, the Prophet said, "One of the rights of a believer over his believing brother is to be called by the name he loves most." This is why giving a beautiful epithet is *Sunna,* in accordance with the Prophet's example. Some of the Companions had such *kunya,* or respectful but intimate names. Most societies have such epithets. But any kind of derogatory term of abuse should be avoided. Calling someone by a derogatory name is *fisq,* or deviant, immoral behavior, so a person doing this is considered to be ignoring the ethics of Islam. This is a very serious situation for anyone to find themselves in. Knowing that this brings serious punishment and a state that is less than true practice and belief, one should actively and carefully avoid calling other people names or mocking them.[42]

MAKING A MOCKERY OF FAITH

Another related topic addressed in the Qur'an is a type of hypocrisy. This occurs when people act one way while with believers, but make fun of the believers when they are not with them, thus showing their hidden identity. Just as believers should not make fun of one another, they should also exercise common sense and avoid making themselves the butt of others' jokes by speaking of their beliefs among people who may mock them once they leave. In Sura Baqara it is written:

> When they meet those who believe, they declare (hypocritically), "We believe"; but when they are alone in secret with their (apparently human) satans (to whom they hasten in need to

renew their unbelief and their pledge to them for fear of losing
their support), they say, "Assuredly we are with you; we only
mock (those others)." (Since what they do only means
demanding straying and ridicule,) God returns their mockery,
leaving them to wander blindly on in their rebellion. Such are
the ones who have bought straying in exchange for guidance,
but their trade has brought no profit, and they have no way
out to escape it. (Baqara 2:14–16)

There is no question about how despicable this kind of behavior is morally; such people cannot be called believers. They show a
friendly, fawning face toward believers while they are with them,
but only so that they can hide their true, malicious intentions.
Then when they get together with the evildoing mischief-makers,
they say, "We are truly with you and were only acting; trust us."
The more they swear their allegiance, the more they are actually
confirming their treachery, pitting themselves against the believers
with their fellow conspirators. Such an action is against basic decency and morality, as these people are mocking and devaluing belief itself; thus, it is easy to understand why such an attitude is one
of the markers of unbelief (*kufr*).

To ridicule someone, even in jest, means to violate their hon-
or and dignity. Most people who make fun of believers do not
have the courage to insult them; if they do, then insult reflects
badly on the person uttering it, not on the one they are insulting.
But when people insult believers, God and the whole universe will
hold them in contempt, whether they realize it or not, even if they
think that their action is concealed. Without a doubt it must be
the greatest burden to have such a thing on one's conscience.[43]

SHOWING OFF

T here are five places in the Qur'an where the word *riya*, or "ostentation," is mentioned. In two of these verses Muslims are warned about people who give charity solely to be seen and regarded. Two others make it known that there are some people who perform daily prayers or other forms of worship just as an outward show. The last of the five teaches that there are some who will claim to be acting out of religious zeal but really only want to put on a show for other people, and we are told what we should do about this. God says in Sura Baqara,

> Those who spend their wealth in God's cause and then do not follow up what they have spent with putting (the receiver) under obligation and taunting, their reward is with their Lord, and they will have no fear, nor will they grieve. A kind word and forgiving (people's faults) are better than almsgiving followed by taunting. God is All-Wealthy and Self-Sufficient, (absolutely independent of the charity of people), All-Clement (Who shows no haste in punishing.) O you who believe! Render not vain your almsgiving by putting (the receiver) under an obligation and taunting—like him who spends his wealth to show off to people and be praised by them, and believes not in God and the Last Day. The parable of his spending is that of a rock on which there is soil; a heavy rain falls upon it, and leaves it barren. They have no power (control) over what they have earned. God guides not such disbelieving people (to attain their goals). (Baqara 2:262–4)

Below are listed the many elements found in this verse:

1. When one gives charity (*sadaqa*), it is invalid and worthless in God's eyes if the giver acts as though the receiver is in-

debted for the gift, or says something to them which will make them uncomfortable.

2. It is clearly commanded that believers must avoid such a situation (when they give charity).

3. The verse makes it known that, when charity is given to prompt gratitude or indebtedness, or to raise one's degree over the receivers of one's charity, or without belief in God and the Last Day, giving only for human recognition, then the money is given in vain and will never benefit the giver.

4. Such a person's situation is compared to a rock face that is covered with a thin layer of dust easily washed away by the rain.

Let us dwell for a moment on this image. As is known, one of the fundamental goals of *sadaqa* or *zakat* (the annual charity every Muslim gives from their accumulated wealth) is to break down the "walls" between the rich and poor, and give assistance to the latter. Thus, even non-material support, such as a kind word or forgiveness of a wrong can be charity, and can be better than money given for the wrong reason (such as the desire to "indebt" the receiver.) The comparison is apt: Just as stone covered with dust will be exposed naked when the rain comes, a person with no belief in God and the Judgment Day who gives charity for show has a heart of stone. This will be exposed at the Final Reckoning.

The following verse also says that such people do not love God, but rather they will become friends of Satan: "*And those who spend their wealth (in charity or other good cause) to make a show of it to people (so as to be praised by them) when they believe neither in God nor in the Last Day: Whoever has Satan for a comrade, how evil a comrade he is!*" (Nisa 4:38).

Another verse regarding ostentation in the Qur'an is this: "*The hypocrites would trick God, whereas it is God who "tricks" them (by causing them to fall into their own traps). When they rise to do the Prayer, they rise lazily, and to be seen by people (to show them that they are Muslims); and they do not remember God (within or outside the*

Prayer) save a little" (Nisa 4:142). One of the main themes of this verse is that a person who acts in such a way does not believe completely in God, the Prophets, the angels, or the Last Day; this makes them *munafiq*, or hypocrites. It depicts them doing their prayers and worship for commendation instead of sincerely. Two aspects of this description catch our attention:

1. Such people do daily prayers only in congregation, and they do them reluctantly.
2. When they do perform the prayers it is because they want people to like them; they lengthen their prostrations so others will see.

A similar verse about hypocrites is from Sura Maun: "*And woe to those worshippers (denying the Judgment), those who are unmindful in their Prayers, those who want to be seen and noted (for their acts of worship), yet deny all assistance (to their fellowmen)*" (Maun 107:4–7). Here I would like to include the commentary of the scholar Elmalili Hamdi Yazir on these verses. According to Yazir, the word *riya* (ostentation and showing off) has several meanings:

1. Doing something, like daily prayers, not for the sake of God, but for some worldly goal.
2. Doing prayers in places where people will see one, but neglecting them in private (when one is alone).
3. Doing the prayers without God-consciousness, simply going through the motions and not thinking of God.

Now let us refer to the following verses from Sura Anfal which clarify the meaning:

> O you who believe! When you meet a host in battle, stand firm and remember and mention God much, that you may triumph. And obey God and His Messenger, and do not dispute with one another, or else you may lose heart and your power and energy desert you; and remain steadfast. Surely, God is with those who remain steadfast. Be not like those (unbelievers) who went forth from their habitations swaggering boastfully and to show off to people, and bar (others) from God's

way. And God fully encompasses (with His Knowledge and Power) all that they do. (Anfal 8:45–47)

There are several layers of meaning in these verses, but the relevant point is that doing things for show, swaggering boastfully, exceeding the bounds of decent interaction, and turning people away from the path of God are all forms of behavior that must be avoided in every arena of society, including cultural, political, economic, and intellectual fields. In other words, we are commanded in all types of conflicts to:

1. Stand firm,
2. Engage often in remembrance of God,
3. Obey God and His Messenger,
4. Avoid dissention and dispute between Muslim communities,
5. Remain patient,
6. Avoid showing off and conceit.

THE SUBJECT OF OSTENTATION IN THE HADITH

It would be appropriate to examine some hadith regarding the subject of hypocrisy here. The Prophet called *riya*, or doing things for show, "lesser *shirk*."[44] One day, according to a narration, he said to the Companions, "The thing I fear most for you is lesser *shirk*." So the Companions asked, "O Messenger of God, what is lesser *shirk*?" He answered, "It is *riya*. It is doing worship to be seen by others. On the Last Day, when God is giving everyone what they deserve, He will say to those who worshipped to be seen by others, 'Go to those you showed off for in the world. See whether they will be able to give you anything now.'"[45]

According to Shaddad ibn Aws, another time God's Messenger said, "I fear for my community two things: *shirk* and hidden lust." So they asked him, "O Messenger of God! After you, would your community ascribe partners to God?" He answered, "Yes; they will not worship the sun, the moon, rocks or idols (like some ancient people), but they will (commit *shirk* when they) do deeds for show."⁴⁶

There are more narrations in which hypocrisy is called "lesser *shirk*," in addition to some *hadith qudsi*. Abu Hurayra heard the Prophet say, "God Almighty says, 'I am completely removed from the partnership ascribed to Me (by those who commit *shirk*). When a person does an action and ascribes it to someone else besides Me, I reject both the ascriber and the one they do the action for.'"⁴⁷ The next hadith is illuminating because it reveals how a person can be found wanting at the Final Reckoning, having fallen into the trap of desiring the acclaim and admiration of others as their goal, and thereby corrupting their intentions: "On Judgment Day, the first person to be brought into God's presence for judgment will be the person who fell as a martyr. God will remind him of the blessings bestowed on him, he will remember them and acknowledge them, and then God will say, 'So, what did you do in return for these blessings?' He will answer, 'I fought for Your cause until I fell as a martyr.' But God will say, 'You are lying. You fought so that the people would say of you, 'What a brave man!' and they said so.' Then He will give the command and the person will be thrown headfirst into Hell.

"The next person to be tried will be a scholar who taught and recited the Qur'an. God will remind him of the blessings bestowed on him, he will remember them and acknowledge them, and then God will say, 'So, what did you do in return for these blessings?' The man will answer, 'I sought knowledge, I taught and I recited the Qur'an for Your sake.' But God will reply, 'You are lying. You learned so that the people would call you "scholar," and you read the Qur'an so they would say "How beautifully he recites." And they did say so.' Then He will give the command and this man too will be thrown headfirst into Hell.

"Then another person will be brought before the Judgment seat: a man who was given all kinds of worldly possessions and opportunities. God will remind him of the blessings bestowed on him, he will remember them and acknowledge them, and then God will say, 'So, what did you do in return for these blessings?' He will say, 'I never begrudged or withheld something You would want me to give, and I gave for Your sake, and spent it for Your pleasure.' But God will say, 'You are lying. All of this, you did so that the people would say, "What a generous man!" And they did say so.' Then He will give the command and this man too will be thrown headfirst into Hell."[48]

Is it always dangerous then for other people to say "What a generous man (or woman)!" of others? Or is the fundamental danger the temptation to enjoy the praise in one's heart, and then to start trying to earn it? The latter is the greater danger; the following hadith shows that great problems can occur when a person is exposed to the praise of others, even when they did *not* wish to seek acclaim. When the Prophet was asked, "O Messenger of God! What do you think about the community praising someone when he does something good?" he answered, "This is payment in advance for a believer."[49] Having examined the Qur'anic verses and hadith on the topic, now let us briefly touch on the teachings of al-Ghazali. According to Imam Ghazali, one form of *riya* is to worship God for the sake of people, to try to deceive or impress them. He also addresses these issues as subtopics:

1. Ostentation in possessions. This type of *riya* is ostentatious clothing, huge houses, garish decorations, and so on. This is inclusive of one's wish to be admired for worldly possessions and achievements, but even worse still is to show off in matters of religion.

2. Ostentation in behavior. For example, lengthening one's prayers and prostrations in the hopes that others will see you; hinting that one's face has gone yellow (looks sickly) because of pious fear of the Last Judgment; trying to make others think one has lost weight because of eating little as a spiritual discipline; trying to appear disheveled to make people think one is busy with religious activities and ser-

vice, and so on. This category of behavior also includes arrogance, swaggering, belittling others, and the like.

According to Ghazali, ostentation and showing off in religion can take three basic forms:

1. Doing actions directly for the sake of being seen to do them. This is the most dangerous category.

2. Wanting to reach a goal through *riya*. This could be a material, immaterial or any type of goal. For example, trying to reach a goal hypocritically by deceiving the community with a sham of "uprightness" or harboring hatred for different people behind the facade of love for the community.

3. Pretending to believe something one does not believe or performing worship just for others to see (while not actually caring about religious precepts), or performing it in a more serious manner when others are watching.

The clearest sign of showing off and ostentation, particularly in worship, is wanting to be seen by people. This indicates attention not to God (Whom one is supposed to be worshipping), but to the people. However, a true worshipper will not care whether or not others know that they are worshipping.[50]

OSTENTATION AND EXCEPTIONAL CIRCUMSTANCES

Bediüzzaman Said Nursi, one of the most influential scholars of Islam in modern Turkey, wrote that some actions, like worship, are not considered to be ostentation, even when done publicly. Generally, he divides acts of worship into two types—*musbat*, or positive, and *manfi*, or negative. The former are those acts of worship we perform regularly, and the latter are the praise and supplications offered when people are afflicted with misfortune or disease, when they think of God and call on Him for help. Since, perceiving their own weaknesses and helplessness, they turn to and seek refuge in their Compassionate Lord, concentrating upon Him and entreating Him alone, this is a pure and sincere form of worship that no hypocrisy or showing off to people can penetrate.[51]

Nursi further states that practices known as *sha'air*, or the symbols of Islam, like the call to prayers, the congregational prayers of Jumu'ah and the two Eids, sacrifice, and so on, that identify Islam and the Muslim community should not be thought of as ostentation. Particularly, there are certain duties that fall on the whole community which can be considered to have been fulfilled if one person performs them; if no one completes this action, then the whole community has neglected an obligatory act. Therefore, when someone performs such a deed, far from being "ostentation," it should be announced and it is a good deed on behalf of the community.[52] Nursi goes into more detail about this topic in his work *Kastamonu Lahikası*, giving a fuller explanation. "There is no *riya*, or ostentation, in performing obligatory or recommended acts, following the example of the Prophet, or avoiding what is forbidden. However, if a person with weak faith intends to do *riya* in performing these acts, (only) then *riya* can occur."

According to such eminent scholars as al-Ghazali, in fact, doing an act that has been designated as obligatory practice openly may carry much greater rewards than doing it in private. Allowing the community to see such practices in a time when the *Sunna* of the Prophet has been lost would not be showing off, but would rather be of benefit to the community. Therefore, to perform such acts publicly would be many times more valuable than performing them privately.[53] Nursi considers any religious responsibility that is carried out with solemnity as being free of ostentation as long as this situation is not abused. For example, when a muezzin who is charged with the task proclaims the call to the prayer or leads the *dhikr* (remembrance of God), loud enough for the congregation to follow, this is not ostentation.[54] Nursi also points out that dissatisfaction and ingratitude can open the door to hypocrisy. On the other hand, *qina'a*, or contentment, frugality, and temperance, closes the door to hypocrisy and ostentation, opening the door to sincerity.[55]

Fethullah Gülen, another one of the greatest Islamic scholars of our age, indicates that it would be wrong to think that someone else is just "acting for show," as no one has any way of measuring this. He insists that we should be harsh with our own self, but when it comes to others, we should practice the Islamic principle of *husn al-zann*, or having good opinion about them.[56]

Gülen also adds that there are many forms of ostentation, including intellectually showing off, such as trying to have one's name mentioned in as many books or bibliographies as possible. He explains that there are some people who may seem humble but who are actually not, as they show signs of ostentation by acting differently when they are in the company of those who are lower in social standing than themselves. Acting in an ostentatious manner belies the "humility" they display. Gülen believes that the hypocrisy of ostentation is everywhere today; prizes and acclaim, awards and plaques, clapping and cheering—he counts them all as dishonest, as examples of ostentation.[57]

TRUSTWORTHINESS

T rust and confidence are two of the most famous characteristics of Prophet Muhammad, peace and blessings be
upon him, from his childhood through his later years as a
Prophet. Everyone, including unbelievers, called him "Muhammad
the Trustworthy." It can be said that those who are trusted by others are assured Paradise, for the Prophet said that such a person
would certainly enter Heaven.

Abu Said narrates, "God's Messenger said, 'If a person eats
lawful, wholesome food and acts according to my example, and
the people feel confident that no wrong will come to them from
that individual, he or she is going to Heaven.'" Upon hearing this,
a Companion said, "O Messenger of God! There are many people
like that living today!" And he replied, "There will also be many
in the times to come!"[58]

In this hadith we are given to understand that a person who
has internalized the ethics of trustworthiness and keeping the confidence of others in their heart and soul, if this is reflected by the
trust they have won from the people around them, is among "the
best of people." As narrated by Abu Hurayra, the Messenger said
one day, "Shall I not tell you who among you is the best and who
among you is the worst?" He repeated this three times. The people who were gathered there said, "Tell us!" He said, "The best of
you are those from whom good is expected, and from whom no
harm is feared. The worst of you are those from whom no good is
hoped and from whom harm is feared."[59]

In the following hadith we can see how critical it is in the
sight of God that this trustworthiness and reliability are developed
in the inner character. Abu Hurayra reports that God's Messenger

said, "Pray to God with certainty that your prayer will be accepted. Know that God does not accept the prayer of a heedless heart (which does not believe in God's trustworthiness), nor a heart that is distracted by other matters."[60]

It bears repeating that in trade and business this principle of being trustworthy and deserving the confidence of others is particularly important. If people who are involved in business remain upright, honest and trustworthy in their dealings, this is like a guarantee of their salvation.

Abu Said al-Khudri said that the Messenger of God instructed, "Traders who do not swerve from uprightness and trustworthiness will be together with the Prophets, the truthful, the martyrs and the righteous."[61] These four classes of people in this hadith correspond with those mentioned in the following Qur'anic verses:

> Whoever obeys God and the Messenger (as they must be obeyed), those are (and in the Hereafter will be, in Paradise) in the company of those whom God has favored (with the perfect guidance)—*the Prophets*, and *the truthful ones* (loyal to God's cause and truthful in whatever they do and say), and *the witnesses* (those who see the hidden Divine truths and testify thereto with their lives), and *the righteous ones* (in all their deeds and sayings and dedicated to setting everything right). How excellent they are for companions! Such is the grace that is from God, and God suffices as One All-Knowing (of how great that grace is, who deserves it, and the rank of those favored with it). (Nisa 4:69–70)

So, an upright, trustworthy business person is like these four classes of people who are *"favored"* with perfect guidance. Such people always prove their trustworthiness by fulfilling their responsibilities which can be either material or non-material such as keeping secrets that have been entrusted to them.

KEEPING SECRETS

P rophet Muhammad, peace and blessings be upon him, took care to instill in children the etiquette of keeping secrets that had been entrusted to them. This lesson is important both for the child's young life and future life, for developing maturity, and for the peace and safety of their family and community. A child who learns how to keep secrets also gains stronger willpower. Such a child can bridle their tongue, and will have less difficulty in hard times, being brave and reliable. This characteristic also inspires confidence in society.

One day Anas, who was a young servant in the Prophet's household, was late in returning to his mother. So she asked him, "Why are you late?" He replied, "God's Messenger sent me to take care of something." His mother asked, "What was it?" But Anas said, "I am to keep it secret." On receiving this answer his sagacious mother said, "In that case, do not tell any secret of God's Messenger to anyone!"[62]

A secret is like an invincible army. It is akin to reputation and honor; one who guards a secret—whether it be their own or someone else's—is guarding their integrity and thus their honor. The one who reveals a secret exposes their honor and dignity to shame, failing to properly esteem them. Likewise, when a person is going to entrust a secret to someone else, they should be as careful and sensitive as if they were entrusting their honor to another. A secret should never be entrusted to one who has an insufficient understanding of honor; to do so is to put a valuable thing in the hands of one who cannot protect it.

Being able to keep a secret, whether one's own or another's, is a human virtue that is related to willpower and comprehension.

Just as someone whose will is weak cannot be expected to keep a secret, a person who cannot comprehend the consequences of their own words or actions is not discreet enough to be told secrets. While it is good on occasion to talk about what is happening in our lives, it is important to avoid pouring out our heart's secrets needlessly. Those who injudiciously broadcast that which is hidden in their hearts risk being swept into danger one day when they say something that cannot be taken back; they should not underestimate this danger to both themselves and their community.

Every individual should be extremely careful about revealing personal and intimate things about themselves, particularly if these are repugnant or ungracious things which can bring no benefit to anyone. Doing so may create unbecoming situations which can embarrass friends and delight enemies. Some secrets involve individuals, others, the family, and still others, the community and even the nation. To reveal a personal secret is to compromise personal honor, to betray a family secret is to endanger family honor, and to divulge a national secret is to jeopardize national honor. As long as a secret is kept to oneself, it brings power to the keeper; but once it is given to others, it becomes a weapon that can be used against the one who revealed it. This is expressed by the Turkish proverb, "A secret is your captive; but if you divulge it, you become its captive."

AVOIDING THE EVILS OF THE TONGUE

The Qur'an draws our attention to good and bad words with a parable. A good word is likened to *"a good tree"* which is well-established and lasting with *"its roots holding firm (in the ground) and its branches in heaven. It yields its fruit in every season due by its Lord's leave"* (Ibrahim 14:24–25). On the other hand, a corrupt word is likened to *"a corrupt tree uprooted from upon the earth, having no constancy"* (Ibrahim 14:26).

Honesty and truthfulness in speech are of great importance, since the tongue is the origin of all honesty and righteousness. This is why we should fear our tongue more than the other organs of our body. Sufyan ibn 'Abdullah relates that he asked the Prophet, "Please teach me a practice to follow!" And the Prophet answered, "Say, 'God is my Creator and Sustainer,' then be upright!" So Sufyan then asked, "What part of me should I worry about?" and the Prophet took hold of his own tongue and said, "This!"[63] Likewise, Abu Hurayra relates a narration in which the Messenger of God commanded, "Let a believer in God and the Last Day either speak good or remain silent."[64]

Someone who is used to empty talk or, in other words, speaking about things that do not concern them, can actually lose their salvation. Such a person may perform the daily prayers, observe the fast, and live an Islamic lifestyle, but if they indulge in vain talk, they should be prepared to lose their place in Heaven and possibly face Hellfire.

A hadith narrated by Anas tells us, "A man passed away. Someone said where the Prophet could hear, 'He must be in Heaven!' The Messenger asked, 'How do you know? It could be that he engaged in vain talk, or perhaps he was hoarding wealth and was stingy with charity.'"[65] That empty talk and stinginess are mentioned together here indicates how serious a sin empty talk actually is. Avoiding the errors of the tongue is more than simply avoiding those things that do not concern one personally. For words that we do not even pay attention to, which we do not think will have any consequences, can bring about very important, lasting effects, either to the good or to the bad.

The Prophet said in a hadith narrated from Abu Hurayra, "Sometimes a person may say something that pleases God and, although the person pays no heed to what he has said, God raises his degree in Heaven. And sometimes a person may say something that displeases God and, although the person gives it no importance, God assigns him seventy years in Hell for it."[66] Clearly, it is important to reign in the tongue, as we see in the English proverb, "If you can't say something good, don't say anything at all." In fact, another two hadith go even farther: According to Umm Habiba, the Prophet said "Every word uttered except for the promotion of good or the prevention of evil or remembrance of God is not to the speaker's credit, but against him."[67] And Ibn Umar relates that the Prophet said, "Do not speak too much other than mentioning God. For speaking much except when mentioning God makes the heart hard. Know that those who are farthest from God are those with insensitive, hard hearts."[68]

Another pitfall of the tongue is using rhetoric as a method of persuasion and enticement. Using deceptive words to trick people into doing something they should not do is a serious offense; in a hadith narrated by Abu Hurayra the Prophet states that no amount of worship will be acceptable from someone who does this. A similar tradition is recounted by Ibn Mas'ud: "The Messenger of God said, 'Those who advance with rhetoric are damned!'"[69]

Another of the dangers of the tongue is being quick to argue. The Prophet said, "Do not argue with your brother or sister, do not make jokes they will not like, and do not make promises you cannot fulfill."[70] Instead of an argument which will bring no solution and may damage the relationship between people, one should remember that respect for the viewpoints of others is never in vain. Valuing the opinions of others, being open and willing to listen and share knowledge will prove effective for solving most problems. Therefore, we should ask questions and listen carefully, and be flexible when necessary; this will help us to avoid the dangers of being argumentative.

Those who avoid an argument even when they are in the right, who avoid lies even in jest, and who have good morals are guaranteed a place in Heaven.[71] We must also be careful not to "return evil with evil." In the Qur'an God says,

> God does not like any harsh speech to be uttered save by one who has been wronged (and therefore has the right to express that in appropriate language). God is indeed All-Hearing, All-Knowing. Whether you do some good openly or do it in secret, or pardon an evil (done to you, even though you have the right to legal retaliation, know that) God is All-Pardoning, Ever-Able (to punish or forgive). (Nisa 4:148–9)

This verse teaches that we must be patient, particularly in our moments of anger. Some people are always ready to react negatively to every little thing that displeases them. Such people can easily be overcome by rage and hatred. God tells us not to be like those who become slaves to their uncontrolled feelings of anger; even if they are in the right, they are unable to get along with others and their hearts are full of storms. We are advised to repay evil with good, or at least avoid repaying evil with evil. After all, God Almighty is so forgiving that He constantly sends sustenance even to the most rebellious of people. Therefore if we are lenient and gentle and able to forgive, even at critical moments when we are upset, we have modeled ourselves on God's attributes and allowed His values to penetrate our hearts.

As will be mentioned in detail in the following section that deals with gossiping and spreading rumors, talking about a person who is proud of their shameful acts and who enjoys recounting their sins in front of others is not gossip. Yet it is important to note that, although it is not gossip to say their behavior is wrong, we still should not be rude to such people if we come face to face with them; we should speak kindly to them and behave nicely toward them. It should also be noted that boasting about the sins you have committed to others is another type of sin. Abu Hurayra explains, "The Messenger of God told us, 'All of my community will be forgiven, except those who broadcast their sins. When someone sins in the night, God covers his sin. But in the morning, if the person tells others what he did at night, he has uncovered what God has covered. This is a form of broadcasting sins.'"[72]

Finally, the last point I want to mention here is this. It is common nowadays to hear people writing others off. In gatherings, or just between friends, spouses or relatives, people speak of the behavior of others just as naturally as if they were discussing the weather. Almost everyone sees themselves as being right and assumes others who do differently are wrong, and therefore, they say things like, "There's no good in these people! They're just frauds. They are good for nothing..." and so on. It must be said that it is one thing to speak of a particular wrong in order to correct that person or to solve the problem when necessary, but it is quite another thing to criticize others for no reason; the latter is displeasing to God. While the former arises from a spiritual desire to better the world, the latter is like a virus, an illness that can blind the spirit or even kill it. Such behavior is unIslamic. Abu Hurayra tells us that the Prophet said, "If you hear someone say '(so-and-so) is damned!' be sure that that person himself is more damned than anyone."[73]

GOSSIPING AND TALE BEARING

C oncealing the faults of others and guarding them from slander are great virtues, whereas backbiting or speaking badly about a believer is a grave sin. The Qur'an says,

> Surely your Lord is He Who knows best who is astray from His way, and He knows best those who are rightly guided. So pay no heed to (the desires of) those who persistently deny (God's Message). They wish you to compromise (with them in matters of faith), so they would compromise (with you). Pay no heed to any contemptible oath-maker (who swears much with no consideration of truth, and no will to act on his word); a defamer, circulating slander (in all directions); who hinders the doing of good, transgressor of all bounds (of sense or decency), one addicted to sinning; cruel and ignoble, and in addition to all that, morally corrupt. (Qalam 68:7–13)

According to most commentators, this was revealed in connection with the behavior of Walid ibn Mughira. He served as an example of a whole list of things to avoid: deviating from the straight path, lying, cursing, backbiting or broadcasting the faults of others, standing in the way of good, aggression, being drawn into sin, losing one's honor, and harshness in manner. Ibn Abbas said of him, "We have never seen another person whose faults were named by God Himself like that." One of these bad attributes that Walid ibn Mughira possessed was spreading rumors. He loved to look for people's faults and then would gossip about them. By publicly denouncing him, God calls on all people to avoid this immoral behavior and the trait of seeking to uncover the faults of another.[74]

Now, to return to our topic after that general introduction, it is well known that to spread rumors or gossip about people, and therefore to create resentment or dissension among believers, is prohibited. According to a hadith narrated by Hamman ibn Haris, such an act is enough to prevent a person entering heaven. The hadith says, "I was together with Hudhayfa in the mosque. A man came and sat with us. He said to Hudhayfa (warning him of another man sneaking in a furtive manner), 'This man officiously carries reports and rumors to the chief and retells them.' Upon hearing this Hudhayfa said, loud enough for the man to hear (and urge strongly), 'I heard God's Messenger say, 'One who spreads rumors cannot enter heaven.'"[75]

Tale bearing and repeating talk about someone else is forbidden. For clearly, mentioning anything about a person that he or she would dislike to hear, even if it is true, is a form of gossip. The Companions received instruction from the Prophet on this matter. Abu Hurayra explains, "The Messenger of God said, 'Do you know what backbiting is?' They responded, 'God and His Messenger know best!' So he said, 'It is talking about someone else in a way they would not like!' Then a man who was present asked, 'What if what I say is true (about the person)? Is it still backbiting?' He answered, 'If what you say is true, it is backbiting. And if it is not true, you have slandered the person as well.'"[76] This rule applies to talking about anyone, not only people we know well. Here I will recount a narration from Aisha, the wife of the Prophet, which serves as a warning about the danger of talking about others:

"I once spoke to the Messenger of God about the qualities of Safiyya (another one of his wives). He was unhappy and said, 'Your words were such that if you dropped them into the ocean, they would pollute all its water.'" She added this regarding another incident: "I impersonated someone (to mock them) to God's Messenger. He immediately said, 'I would never impersonate (the faults of) another—not even if I were given a huge treasure to do so!'"[77]

In addition to avoiding gossip and talking about others, a Muslim is also responsible for defending others from being slandered in their presence. Although one who repeats gossip or slanders others may not be punished in this world, we know that they will be after death. The following teaching by Prophet Muhammad, peace and blessings be upon him, reflects this eternal truth. According to Muadh ibn Asad al-Juhani, his father heard this from the Prophet's lips: "Whoever defends a believer against gossip, God will send him an angel on the Last Day to save his body from the fire of Hell. And whoever throws a slanderous accusation on a Muslim's name, God will imprison him on the bridge over Hell on the Last Day until this sin is purified."[78] On the other hand, saying the truth about someone who openly defies religious decrees, who enjoys sinning and broadcasts it publicly is not considered to be gossip. Jabir and Abu Hurayra explain, "God's Messenger said, 'What is said about someone who sins openly is not gossip. My entire community, except those who openly sin, are eligible for forgiveness.'"[79]

AVOIDING AN EVIL ATTITUDE
TOWARD OTHERS

The term *hasad*, which means that one is not comfortable with the blessings of another person, is a feeling of resentment that someone else has a particular possession, attainment, or endowment, wishing that they did not have it or that they lose it.[80] This is one of the worst psychological and spiritual types of immorality that can be found in the human heart. Particularly when combined with ignorance and greed, such feeling of resentment can cause even worse things. In some people this feeling comes and goes in a moment. In others, it takes root, takes over the personality, and grows like cancer. The type of resentment which we will discuss is this latter, the most dangerous one.

Envy that is full of resentment is clearly wrong. But sometimes even *ghibta*, or admiration, can give way to a problematic degree of jealousy. For example, one may admire and esteem a scholar, but later start to think, "Why does he have knowledge and I do not?" If this feeling or thought arises, then the "admiration" has gone too far. There is a fine line between these feelings. It is critical to pay close attention and remain watchful with regard to such feelings.

When a person thinks, "I am a little jealous," they may unwittingly already have begun to harbor feelings of resentment. From this perspective, a believer must be careful not to provoke believing brothers and sisters toward jealousy, while a person who knows that they are prone to jealousy or envy is responsible for controlling it.[81] Feelings of resentment, if a person is aware of them, first of all damage the person in whom the feelings have arisen. If someone who is under the influence of this feeling understands that their resentment arises from seeing the other person receive something good, then they should feel bad about themselves, even if they are a selfish person. They also cause themselves pain because deep within themselves this feeling feeds the desire "not to be deprived"; this is a great burden on a person. Such a person will spend a large part of their energy on making needless comparisons between themselves and others. And what is more, resentment toward other people will strain relationships and act as an obstacle to friendship.

Resentment causes people to lose a healthy perspective on their own life and to neglect their own responsibilities and work. Depending on the degree, resentment can destroy one's morality as well. An envious mind derails a person from the straight path, no matter how good they may appear. However, it is very hard for the person themselves to recognize this. One who nurtures such grudges resents the blessings of others merely because they do not possess the same. This sickness cannot coexist with true piety, righteousness, justice, good sense, and virtues.

Imam Ghazali defines *hasad* as a feeling that is opposed to the blessings of another person. Ghazali says that when God grants someone a blessing the people around them can react in one of two ways:

1. They think the blessing is excessive and want the person to lose it. This is *hasad*; the sign of such resentment is the desire that the person no longer has the possession in question or being happy when they lose it.

2. They may have no positive or negative feelings about the thing granted to the other person; they do not wish for it to be lost. The opposite of this is *ghibta*, that is, the desire that one is given the same thing without desiring that it should pass away from the other person who has it.

The first reaction, when one does not like to see others granted a blessing and wishes for it to be taken away, is designated as being *haram* (forbidden) and is decried in the strongest terms by Islamic scholars. There is one exception: it is not a sin to wish that a blessing be taken away if the immoral and sinful recipient is using it to instigate strife among people, or using it as an excuse to oppress people; the cause of dislike in such a case is not envy of the good thing that person has, but the desire that the ability to cause such injustice and strife should not be with such an evil person.[82]

THE SUBJECT OF *HASAD* IN THE QUR'AN

In the Qur'anic verses that deal with this feeling of resentment there is a general distinction between two types of *hasad*—that of individuals and that of societies. Here these two varieties of resentment will be discussed and we will look at how we can protect ourselves against each of them.

> If anything good happens to you, this grieves them; if any misfortune befalls you, they rejoice at it. Yet if you endure and persevere in your way and act in piety keeping from evil and any injustice, their guile will never harm you. Surely God fully encompasses (with His Knowledge and Power) all that they do. (Al Imran 3:120)

In the above verse the following ideas have been laid out:

1. Unbelievers who harbor enmity against religion and believers and who wish that believers do not receive any good things from their Lord are greatly grieved and frustrated when the believers are blessed.

2. Similarly, the abovementioned people love to see disaster visited upon the religion and religious people.

3. People who hate believers will also work secretly to prevent them from attaining something good or to cause them trouble.

God has shown us ways to avoid the wiles of such enemies and to protect ourselves against their plots. The verse shows us two basic ways to protect ourselves against them:

1. Strength of patience should be exercised in the face of any cruelty, oppression, or unjust treatment inflicted on us by sinful people or unbelievers.

2. We should also take refuge in *God consciousness* and act accordingly by following His commands and avoiding what He has forbidden. Elmalili Hamdi Yazir has this to say in the interpretation of the above verse: "Against all these, the duty of a Muslim is to be patient, and this is their protection. Thus we will not be overcome by their enmity. If a Muslim is patient and perseveres in obeying God's commands and avoiding doing wrong, the traps and intrigues of the unbelievers and hypocrites will never harm them."[83]

The Qur'an also says what will become of those who harbor feelings of resentment and envy:

> Many among the People of the Book, out of the envy ingrained in their souls, wish they could restore you as unbelievers after you have believed, after the truth was clear to them (that the Qur'an is God's Word and Muhammad is the last, awaited Messenger). Yet pardon and overlook them (avoiding useless debates and polemics with them) until God brings in His verdict about them. Surely God has full power over everything. (Baqara 2:109)

God sets forth the following steps for the Muslim community to prevent these negative feelings and behavior:

1. To choose the "high road" of forgiving and forbearing in response to provocative stances and incitement;
2. To maintain basic common ground in interpersonal relationships;
3. To refrain from useless debates and polemics with people until God brings in His judgment about them, enabling a way out for the disputes.

In the Qur'an, God says that Muslim communities should pursue dialogue and try to establish ties with groups that have set themselves against them as enemies:

> So (O Messenger) call people to that (the way of life God has laid down for you). Pursue what is exactly right (in every matter) as you are commanded (by God). Do not follow their

desires and caprices, and say, "I believe in whatever Book God has sent down; and I am commanded to bring about equity among you (without discrimination of race or rank by birth or by wealth or by power). God is our Lord and your Lord. To us are accounted our deeds, and to you, your deeds: (let there be) no contention between us and you: God will bring us all together (and settle any difference between us and you). To Him is the homecoming." (Shura 42: 15)

The verse shows the necessary approach in nine parts:

1. Whatever happens, continue to exhort people who are opposed to you and invite them to good.
2. It is necessary for the Muslim community to obey and follow the commands and prohibitions it has been given.
3. It is critical not to follow the whims of those who oppose you, nor the ideas of those who believe that strife, discord, and estrangement are the normal state of humankind.
4. It is the sign of a believer to have faith in everything God has put forth in His revelations, in every Scripture He has sent down.
5. It is essential to judge between all people equally and fairly.
6. God is the Lord and Creator of all, whether or not they believe in Him.
7. Every community is responsible for what it does, and every individual will bear their own responsibility; they will not be responsible for the sins of other people.
8. Every person will answer for what they do and, as God will judge them, people should avoid unnecessary arguments.
9. God will be the One to call everyone to account for what they have done.

PROTECTING ONESELF AGAINST THE ILL WILL OF OTHERS

Now let us look at ways that we can be saved from the ill will of others. The following verse commands that we seek refuge with God from "the evil of" four things:

Say, "I seek refuge in the Lord of the daybreak from the evil of what He has created, and from the evil of the darkness (of night) when it overspreads, and from the evil of the witches who blow on knots (to cast a spell), and from the evil of the envious one when he envies." (Falaq 113:1–5)

Naturally, the one that applies to our subject here is the last one, envy. Actions produced by a heart that is filled with hatred can affect the person against whom harm is desired; we all know that a certain degree of envy can lead a person to physically attack another person. But we also know that under no circumstances can any harm or help come to a person without God's permission. Further, if harm touches us, no one besides God can ward it off. So, taking refuge in God is the only way to be protected against evil.

These are the precautions that can be taken against *hasad*:

1. We must be patient with the one who bears us envy, and not sink to their level by losing our temper.

2. No matter if the antagonist does not fear God, nor feel shame before people, or acts in disgraceful, unfair ways, the one being antagonized should never be tempted to waver from belief and justice.

3. The antagonist should not be given too much attention or thought about too much. To dwell on such a person is the first step to allowing them to defeat one.

4. Do not inflict any ill treatment against the antagonist. Forgive them, and if you have the chance, do good to them. Do not pay any attention to the bad things they think about you.

5. Persevere and rely on God when confronted with resentment. When trust in God has truly taken root in a person's heart that person no longer fears anyone else.[84]

THE SUBJECT OF *HASAD* IN THE HADITH

Now we will take a look at the words of our Prophet, peace and blessings be upon him, on the topic of *hasad*. Anas ibn Malik reported that when among the Companions one day the Messenger of God said, "The man who is about to come in is deserving of Heaven." Just then, an Ansari man with water dripping from his beard from his ablutions came in, holding his shoes in his left hand. The next day, the Prophet said the same thing. Then the same man came in. On the third day the Prophet said this a third time and the same man entered again. When the Prophet left, 'Abdullah ibn Amr went to the Ansari man and asked if he could stay at his house for a few days. After his stay he said this about what he had seen: "I was in his house for three nights. But I did not see him get up at night to pray. I heard him mention God whenever he woke up, until the morning prayer time. And he never spoke of anything but good the entire time. After three days I was starting to think he did not do anything special (enough to deserve such commendation of the Prophet). I asked him, 'God's Messenger told us three times, "The man who is about to come in is deserving of Heaven," and each time you came in. I wanted to stay with you to see what good deeds you are doing. But I have not seen anything out of the ordinary. What is it that elevates you to the level the Prophet talked about?' The man said, 'I do only what you have seen.' So I turned around to leave, but as I was leaving he called, 'But I should add, I never hold any enmity or hatred towards any Muslim in my heart. Thanks to the goodness of God I have never harbored envy toward anyone.'" On hearing this, 'Abdullah said, "Ah! This is what has lifted you to such a high degree."[85]

According to Zubayr, the Prophet said, "The sicknesses of ancient societies have spread to you: envy and hatred. These can denude you of your religion and your faith. By God Almighty, Who holds my soul in His hand, you cannot enter Heaven without having faith. And you cannot have faith without loving each other. Shall I tell you something that will help you to love each other? Spread the peace greeting amongst yourselves."[86]

Another hadith from Ibn Mas'ud reports that the Prophet said, "It is not permissible to envy anyone except in two cases: one who makes a judgment with wisdom that has been given to them by God and who teaches this wisdom to others; one who spends their God-given material possessions in the Way of God."[87]

Anas also narrated the following hadith from God's Messenger: "Envy inevitably eats up blessings and good, just as fire consumes wood. Charity (*sadaqa*) covers errors, just as water puts out fire. The daily prayers are the Light of the believer. And fasting will protect you from the Flame (of Hell)."[88]

Yet another narration of the Prophet relays these words: "The believer has four enemies: another believer who harbors envy; a hypocrite who is in a rage; Satan, who diverts them from the right path; the disbeliever who attacks them."[89]

Abu Said al-Khudri also transmitted a hadith in which Gabriel came to the Messenger of God and said, "O Muhammad, are you sick?" and when he said yes, the angel read this prayer: "I invoke the name of God for you, against all sicknesses that pain you, against all evil souls and against envious eyes. In the name of God, I pray that God may heal you."[90]

We can come to the following conclusions from this hadith:

a. One of the most important factors indicating whether a person will be admitted to Heaven since it is a sign and manifestation of perfect faith—is a heart and soul free of resentment toward others and envy for material and non-material blessings.

b. Even if one cannot completely eliminate feelings of resentment toward someone, one must strive to treat them with fairness and consideration, never doing wrong to them, and containing the feelings so they do not overflow their boundaries.

c. It is essential to try to protect oneself from this mischievous inclination, recalling that it can cancel out and destroy one's good deeds "just as fire destroys wood."

d. One who believes in God, the Prophets, the Scriptures, and the pillars of faith sincerely should remember that it is not right for a believer to resent or hate others because they have been blessed with material or spiritual riches. To do so is to resent God Almighty's decision and judgment. A person who recognizes this malice in themselves should realize that their faith is in danger and take measures to clean and protect their heart from the damage this can cause.

e. When someone else looks or acts hatefully toward us, and if we think we have been affected by it or even made ill by it, it is best to take refuge in God Almighty and pray to Him for protection, health, and healing.

In short, *hasad* is one of the most serious spiritual illnesses that can infect the human breast. Spiritual ills can only be cured by knowledge and action. In order to cure this malice, it is critical to be aware of the dangers that it poses to one's faith and to the world; knowledge is the first line of defense. In order to want to be free of envy, one must truly understand the full import of it.

To harbor spite and resentment means that a person has set themselves against the will and decision of God, and that they are ungrateful for what He has apportioned them. Moreover, harboring such ill feelings is paramount to refusing to believe that there is hidden wisdom behind these decisions; this in turn goes against *tawhid*, overturning it, and threatening basic faith. As Bediüzzaman Said Nursi said, "Whoever criticizes Divine Determination is striking their head against an anvil on which it will break (i.e., by criticizing it, one only hurts oneself) and whoever objects to Divine Mercy will be deprived of mercy."[91]

Neutralizing *Hasad*

Now let us briefly examine some ways that *hasad* can be expunged from the heart.

1. In order to eliminate this ill feeling, merely being aware of the true extent of its destructive nature is enough. However, in addition, it should also be remembered that one who harbors *hasad* against a believer becomes guilty of further sins: these can include cheating a believer, refusing to give them good advice, becoming a bad example by not practicing Islam properly, and becoming a tool of Satan by being gladdened at the losses of others. The seriousness of this sin cannot be underestimated. In other words, as we saw above, it is a sickness that destroys the purity and sincerity of the heart, as well as its good feelings and good deeds.[92]

2. A constant fire burns within the heart that harbors hatred and this will eventually consume that person. For resentment that is born of envy increases as the object of envy continues to receive blessings, until the envious person's heart contracts; they start to lose sleep as they fall into the grip of this deadly disease. This is a condition one's enemies rejoice to see. As Bediüzzaman Said Nursi wrote, envy oppresses and destroys the envious one, not the one who is envied. The feeling of resentment will barely touch the one who is envied, not affecting them at all.[93] Thus, the intelligent thing to do is to realize that all accounts will be settled at the end of time as God is the Ultimate Judge, and to try to be freed from *hasad*, which is a useless emotion. In truth, *hasad* itself will be punished on the Last Day too, so meditating on the Judgment is helpful in more than one way.[94]

3. Another way to cure the "sickness" of *hasad* is to refuse to carry out the negative actions that are urged by these feelings—in fact, by doing just the opposite we can gain mastery over such emotions. This means that we should recognize that by doing wrong to the person we feel resentment or hatred against we are falling into a trap that has been set for us by Satan; knowing this, we should force ourselves to overcome our ego and do good to these people instead.

This means that when feelings of resentment impel us to act in an unpleasant manner with those we dislike, we must fight this feeling and be humble instead. Again, if these negative feelings cause us to want to be miserly with them, we should be generous in spite of our feelings. Acting in this way will both eliminate these negative emotions as well as creating another effect. The other person will feel happy and think well of us. This can actually create affection and, with time, eradicate the sickness of resentment and envy. Although these actions at first are difficult to carry out, with practice they become second nature, a part of one's personality. Of course, this situation will not please Satan and he will try to interfere in these positive developments. He may inspire in us feelings of distrust of any good action on the part of the other person, thus putting doubts and fears into our minds. However, a believer will know that these are just the whispers of Satan, the Accursed One, and that he and his designs will come to naught. By making an effort to do good to the person we can seek refuge in God and ask for patience.[95]

4. It does not befit a believer to tie their heart to passing things in this temporary world; therefore, there is no reason for a believer to feel slighted when these things belong to others and not to them. It may help to restore a balanced perspective to remember that God's eternal blessings are far more valuable than the fleeting material possessions of this world. This can go a long way in helping abate resentment.

5. Someone who feels resentment stirring in their heart should make sure that they do not manifest it outwardly; this requires discipline. Indeed, if we "let resentment out" we will grow accustomed to it; this is not something that we can allow to happen. Every person must keep their own hands, mouth, eyes, tongue, and ears under control at all times.[96]

SAFEGUARDING THE GOOD
NAME OF OTHERS

The Qur'an enjoins believers to refrain from indulging in unfounded suspicion, searching for faults, and speaking ill of others:

> O you who believe! Avoid much suspicion, for some suspicion is a grave sin (liable to God's punishment); and do not spy (on one another), nor backbite (against one another). Would any of you love to eat the flesh of his dead brother? You would abhor it! Keep from disobedience to God in reverence for Him and piety. Surely God is One Who truly returns repentance with liberal forgiveness and additional reward, All-Compassionate (particularly towards His believing servants). (Hujurat 49:12)

The Holy Qur'an points to at least three basic prohibitions in this verse:

1. One should not presume bad things about others, or think poorly of them.
2. One should not pry into the private business of others.
3. One should not say negative things about others behind their backs—in other words, one should not gossip about them.

Now let us try to understand these three major ideas in the verse, one at a time.

1. *Assuming the Best:* There are different types of assumptions. In Islam "assuming someone is good," or having a good opinion and thinking well of others is known as *husn al-zann*, while "assuming someone is bad," or thinking bad about others is called *su' al-zann*. *Husn al-zann*, or having good thoughts about others, should be our goal; we should think good of, first of all, God, then God's

Messenger, and then all the believers, and even all human beings. On the other hand, it is sinful to have negative thoughts about others without proof, or to nurture *su' al-zann,* which means disregarding a person's good side and thinking badly about them.

In Islamic teaching it is essential to view others as good unless or until we have seen definite evidence to the contrary. Any person must be presumed good, even if incorrect behavior or bad characteristics are suspected; this is true unless such suspicions are confirmed by evidence. In fact, this is the same principle that guides the legal formula, "innocent until proven guilty," where the burden of proof lies with the accuser, and the accused is blameless until incontrovertible evidence proves them to be guilty. Since the burden of proof is on the accuser, those who cannot prove their assumptions engage in "presumption" or conjecture, which is wrong in both religious and civil laws. The Messenger warned the believers, "Desist from saying 'I think (such-and-such about so-and-so).' For conjecture is the most deceptive (form) of talk."[97]

2. *Avoiding Meddling and Prying:* Safeguarding personal dignity and not prying into the faults of others are important manners that should be observed in social life. In relation to this, God has commanded, *"Do not spy on one another."* In the aforementioned verse, the Arabic word *tajassus,* derived from the verb *jassa,* is used. The meaning of this verb is to dig for information about something, to think about it and to try to comprehend its hidden face.[98] God decrees, "Do not search out shameful things." This is a sensitive subject. Indeed, the Messenger of God warned us about the punishment for such actions: "O you who profess faith with your tongues but do not confirm it with your hearts! Do not torment Muslims, do not pry into their private lives. If you try to uncover the secrets of your Muslim brother, God will uncover your secrets. And whoever seeks for shameful things in others, even if they are in their own house, God will bring them to shame before people."[99] Finding people's hidden faults, bringing them into the open and publicizing them naturally provokes shame in the one who does this, and that shame is a signal from God. The result is that such a person will begin to do publicly things that they used to feel compelled to hide. From the perspective of *akhlaq,* this is an undesirable position. The Prophet said, "If anyone covers the faults of a Muslim, God will cover his faults on the Judgment Day."[100] Thus, we should not pry in an attempt to find out the faults or private affairs of others, but rather strive to conceal their faults.

3. *Avoiding Backbiting:* Islamic scholars agree that backbiting is *haram* (prohibited). It is compared to eating the flesh of a human being: *"...do not backbite (against one another). Would any of you love to eat the flesh of his dead brother? You would abhor it!"* (Hujurat 49:12).

The Companions once asked the Messenger of God, "What if the fault we speak of is one our brother truly has?" He replied, "If the person truly has the fault you speak of, then you are backbiting. And if he does not, then you have slandered him."[101]

Clearly, then, to say something about someone that would upset them if they heard it is backbiting, a great sin. However, if it is not true of them, then it is slander, an even greater sin.

Just as it is prohibited to speak negatively about other people, the person who does not protest when hearing such conversations has also committed a wrong act. If a believer violates this rule but another keeps silent and allows it, that silence is also a form of transgression. Basically, one must not allow oneself to be found in such circumstances, and one should refuse to listen to gossip. The promise of the Messenger of God must not be forgotten: "One who guards the honor and reputation of a sister or brother in Islam in their absence will be rescued by God from the fire of Hell."[102]

VERIFYING WHAT ONE HEARS

From time immemorial it has been the case that blind acceptance of information broadcast among the community has
resulted in numerous misunderstandings, which often lead
to unrest or other serious situations. For this reason the Qur'an tells
us what the proper conduct of a believer is in such matters:

> O you who believe! If some transgressor brings you news (that
> requires taking action), verify it carefully (before you believe
> and act upon it), lest you harm a people in ignorance and then
> become regretful for what you have done. (Hujurat 49:6)

Some scholars believe that this verse was revealed because of an
incident involving Walid ibn Ukba ibn Abu Muayt. There is a tradition which recounts the incident as follows. The Prophet sent Walid
ibn Ukba to collect the *zakat* from some people of the Banu Mustaliq
clan who had accepted Islam. Walid went there, but because he was
afraid, he turned back; he returned to the Prophet and told him that
they had refused to pay *zakat* and threatened to kill him. When the
Prophet heard this he prepared an army to go and quell the supposed rebellion. But before they left, the chief of the Banu Mustaliq,
Harith ibn Dirar, came to the Prophet with a delegation and said,
"We swear before God, we did not refuse to pay *zakat*, nor threaten
to kill the one who came to collect it; we did not even see Walid!
We are still believers and ready to give our *zakat*."[103]

The event that prompted this revelation makes it clear the
general meaning of this verse, with no room for speculation or interpretation. Believers must be very careful that they act on correct
knowledge, particularly in matters that require responsibility and
which are concerned with social relationships. If a person is known
to be someone who does wrong and is not honest, then one must

be very careful about believing what they say. Accepting anything and everything one hears as being true without checking first will, as the verse tells us, unavoidably cause embarrassing or potentially dangerous blunders.

But what exactly is a *fasiq*, the type of person mentioned in the verse? In the early age of Islam, this word denoted someone who still considered himself a believer, but yet engaged in behavior that was forbidden by Islam, overstepping the bounds of what is ethically allowable. As defined by Raghib al-Isfahani, it is "someone who believes but does not follow some of the mandates (of religion)." In other words, for these purposes, a *fasiq* is someone who is not entirely to be trusted because they are known to do unethical or immoral things. Taking at face value any important information that is brought by such a person can lead to a huge disaster. For this reason God tells us that when we hear something very important, we must take into consideration who is telling us this information before immediately believing it; if the bearer of the news is not a completely trustworthy person, then, on principle, the news should be verified before the information is acted upon or before we believe ill of another person or group because of what has been reported.

As this Qur'anic verse shows, a person who is not entirely trustworthy should not be a witness. Indeed, in Islamic law scholars consider the testimony of a *fasiq* invalid, and the evidence of such a person is thus inadmissible in court. As Imam Qurtubi said, "The testimony of a *fasiq* is not valid; for information is like a valuable object which should not be entrusted to just anyone. And (unethical behavior) makes a person unqualified to be entrusted with the truth."[104] It should be noted, however, that one is regarded as trustworthy until such a transgression as lying, slander, or the committing of any prohibited action has been established.

It goes without saying that common sense and balance must be applied; these strictures are for important information, meaning matters when another person's liberty or privacy is in question.

(The word *naba* in the verse is not applied to simple daily information; its meaning is *crucial* information.) People must not go to the other extreme and think it necessary to investigate every single tidbit heard from another person they may not know well, nor try to determine if that person is a *fasiq* before accepting anything they have said. The necessity for verification pertains to serious situations, not day-to-day minor issues.

In short, the verse is stating that generally, when dealing with a person who is known for immorality, we should be careful to check out any serious stories they tell us before forming opinions or taking actions based only on their word. People who are trustworthy, on the other hand, should be believed, since they carry out their duties and are mindful of their responsibilities. Becoming suspicious of news from normal, trustworthy people, doubting everything, or trying to find proof damages the bonds of trust and leads to paranoia. This is an obstacle to personal mental health and the stability of the community.

CHAPTER 4

Promoting Good Character
in Social Life

GREETING

The word *salaam,* or "peace," is a derivative of the verb *salama;* it is a prayer for a peaceful life far from evil and sin. God says in the Qur'an, *"When you are greeted with a greeting (of peace and goodwill), answer with one better, or (at least) with the same. Surely, God keeps account of all things"* (Nisa 4:86).

The Qur'an also clarifies the forms of greetings. Accordingly, Muslims should greet another Muslim by saying *Salaamun 'alaykum* (or *As-salaamu 'alaykum*), meaning "peace be upon you." In the Qur'an both Prophet Muhammad, peace and blessings be upon him, and the angels greet believers in this way.[1]

When a Muslim greets another Muslim this way, the response is, *wa 'alaykum salaam wa rahmatullahi,* meaning "and may peace and the mercy of God be upon you." If the first greeting was *salaamun 'alaykum wa rahmatullah,* meaning "peace and mercy on you," the response should be *wa 'alaykum salaam wa rahmatullahi wa barakatuh,* meaning "and may peace, mercy and blessings be on you." The Messenger taught that this last form of greeting was the one used between Prophet Adam, the first man, and the angels.[2]

To greet each other with this wish for peace is a direct result of friendship and wishing good for others. It is a practice that Muslims take from the life of the Prophet, the *Sunna;* responding to such a greeting is compulsory *(fard).* A hadith says, "Without faith you cannot enter Heaven. And without loving each other you cannot have faith. Shall I show you something to do out of love for each other? Spread the peace greeting between yourselves."[3]

The following are some *adab* guidelines for greeting one another:

1. When entering a gathering, say *salaamun ʿalaykum* before beginning to talk.

2. We can greet by giving salaams when we first see someone and we can also give the same greeting when parting. In fact, God's Messenger said, "If one of you gives a greeting when entering a place, give it when leaving too."

3. When entering a place where there are no people, one should say *as-salaamu ʿalayna wa ʿala ibadillahissalihin* (to greet the unseen beings there).[4]

4. The initiator of greetings should be the younger person (when two people meet, or in general), the smaller party rather than the larger one when at a gathering and those who are walking rather than those who are sitting.

5. When a group is greeted, someone in the group can reply *wa ʿalaykum as-salaam* on behalf of the whole group; however, if no one replies, everyone in the group is remiss in this duty.

6. It is also good to give salaams when leaving a gathering. When this is done, it is best for the one who receives the greeting to reply by saying *wa ʿalaykum as-salaam wa rahmatullahi wa barakatuh*.

7. The *salaam* should be given to everyone, whether we know them.

8. It is also a tradition of the Prophet to say *marhaba* to someone who greets us. *Marhaba* comes from the verb *rahaba*, meaning "be at peace; be comfortable, you are among friends."

9. The response to the greeting should be given immediately, and if possible, loud enough for the greeter to hear.

10. When greeting and replying to a greeting, one's voice should not be too loud or too soft.

11. When giving and receiving a greeting, the tone of voice should convey respect and good will.

There are times when it is inappropriate to give the peace greeting. Below is a list of these:

1. Since "(*As-*)*Salaam*" is also one of God's beautiful Names, meaning "the Supreme Author of peace and salvation," it should not be pronounced in ritually unclean places.

2. This greeting should not be given to a person while they are engaged in something that is *haram*, or forbidden.

3. Someone engaged in reading the Qur'an, recounting a hadith, or teaching should not be greeted, as to do so would be to interrupt these valuable activities. However, when they have finished, they can be greeted.

4. Someone sounding the *adhan* (call to prayer), praying, or reciting the *iqama* (the call at the commencement of the obligatory prayer) should not be greeted.

5. The greeting is to be given between believers. Therefore, someone who rejects Islam should not be greeted with this greeting. But if such a person greets a Muslim, they should reply *wa 'alaykum*.

6. Giving the greeting to those who cannot reply in kind is discouraged.

7. Giving the greeting to anyone who is not ashamed to mention the sins they have committed is discouraged.

8. To give and receive the greeting is a sign of friendship and love. But bowing before another person is discouraged, as Muslims should only bow before God. According to some scholars, bowing when greeting others can be considered to be a form of prostrating before them.

SHAKING HANDS

The word *musafaha* means to squeeze a person's hand and to shake it. In Islam, when two people meet, the most common way of initiating the greeting is to grasp both hands before saying the verbal peace greeting. *Musafaha* can also include kissing the hand (of an elder), kissing a person on both cheeks, or hugging on the right side (so that their hearts are near to one another).

When God's Messenger greeted others (especially before the Friday congregational prayers or Eid prayers), he performed *musafaha*. Islamic scholars unanimously agree that *musafaha* is *Sunna*.[5] The Prophet said something very encouraging about this practice: "When two Muslims meet each other, if they perform *musafaha* and intercede for one another, God Almighty will forgive their sins before they leave that place." According to this hadith, it is essential to do *musafaha* and pray to God that the other person will be forgiven.[6]

Qatada, who was of the second generation after the Prophet asked Anas ibn Malik, one of the Blessed Companions, "Was there *musafaha* between the Companions?" Anas replied "Yes!"[7] Ibn Mas'ud related in a hadith, "(For a Muslim to perform *musafaha* to a fellow Muslim) they should take them by the hand and exchange the peace greeting."[8] This leads us to conclude that greeting each other in this way also dissipates any anger there may be between two hearts.[9]

There are various hadith and traditions regarding the *musafaha* of the Prophet. It is said that he performed *musafaha* every time

he met someone and that he did so with both hands,[10] never re-
moving his hand before the other person withdrew theirs.[11] It is
also said that *musafaha* is the completion of the peace greeting.[12]
In yet another hadith, "If two Muslims greet each other with
musafaha when they meet, their sins will be forgiven." And another added, "Their sins will fall down from their joined hands, and
be taken away."[13] In another related hadith, God's Messenger said,
"Shake hands and rancor will disappear. Give presents to each other and love each other and enmity will disappear."[14]

BREAKING OFF RELATIONS

Resentment and irritability eat away at feelings of brotherhood; it is extremely harmful to nurse grudges. If one is offended by something a fellow Muslim does, it is important to make peace immediately. In the words of the Qur'an, *"The believers are but brothers, so make peace between your brothers and keep from disobedience to God in reverence for Him and piety (particularly in your duties toward one another as brothers), so that you may be shown mercy (granted a good, virtuous life in the world as individuals and as a community, and eternal happiness in the Hereafter)"* (Fussilat 49:10).

The Qur'an tells us that Muslims are brothers and sisters. If two Muslims have a falling-out and remain at odds with each other and if they cannot get over this, what should be done? According to the verse, we are commanded to try to bring these people together to help them overcome the rift. A Muslim should feel compelled to make peace between others as a duty and responsibility. This "brotherhood" of believers in Islam is not meant to be in word only. Just like blood siblings, other believers deserve to be treated well by us, and we are charged with caring for them and seeing to their physical and spiritual needs, giving support and guidance to them when they need it, and staying in touch with them.

The Prophet reminded us that caring for our brothers and sisters is directly related to faith when he said, "One who does not want for his brother what he wants for himself does not have (true) faith."[15] It is not acceptable for a Muslim to remain estranged from another Muslim for more than three days under normal circumstances (barring some legitimate reason). In fact, the Prophet said, "It is forbidden for a Muslim to remain angry with his brother for more than three days. When three days have passed, he should go immediately to the person and greet them; if the greeting is returned, both of them will be rewarded; but if the person does not return the salutation, he will bear the sin and the one who greeted will have emerged from the sin of keeping apart.[16]

When a falling-out has occurred, it is better to be the first to go and make peace with the other. The Prophet said, "It is not permissible for a Muslim to remain estranged from his Muslim brother (because of a falling-out). When they come across each other, one turns his face to one side, the other turns to the other side (to avoid one another). The better of them is the one who speaks first and initiates reconciliation."[17]

It should also be noted, however, that occasionally there may be legitimate reasons for a rift, such as the breaking off relations for the purpose of admonition. For example, a father could tell his grown son, "I will not talk to you until you stop drinking alcohol," in order to prompt him to reform. This would not be the same as refusing to see someone because they have upset you. There is such an example in the life of the Messenger of God: he did not speak to some of the Companions for a time (in Medina) when they did not join a military campaign without any valid excuse. It was not until they finally repented and their repentance was accepted by God Almighty, more than fifty days after the campaign, that the Prophet resumed speaking with them. From this we can infer that there are cases where a compelling reason justifies not speaking to someone.[18]

Nevertheless, if there is no such special reason, remaining estranged from someone out of anger for more than three days is an act of peevishness that arises from the ego or from Satan's promptings. Furthermore, there are important consequences when such a falling-out comes between two believers, and thus this situation should be avoided. The main reasons for not falling out are, in short, to preserve harmony in families as well as outside them, to overcome impulses that lead to aggression or violence, and to protect the spiritual and psychological health of individuals.

When examined closely it is clear that erroneous principles of interaction are what lie behind all dysfunctional family or community relationships. One of these faulty principles is allowing resentment or rifts to fester and remain unresolved. Such feelings undermine trust between people. It is a well-recognized fact that in day-to-day relationships, be they at work, at home, or with a spouse, trust is of the essence. It is necessary to constantly renew and build up these bonds of trust by letting resentment go. It is easy to understand that resentment can develop into aggressive and even violent feelings. The following hadith emphasizes the importance of eliminating this possibility by speedy reconciliation. According to Abu Hurayra, the Prophet said, "Every Monday and Thursday God reviews our deeds. On those days, God Almighty forgives all His servants who are not in *shirk*. The only exception is brothers (or sisters) in faith who remain in conflict with each other; (they are not forgiven) until they make peace with each other."[19] This hadith indicates that holding a grudge can worsen, or at least continue, a state of antagonism toward a brother or sister in faith.

PRAYING FOR BLESSINGS UPON SNEEZING

When a Muslim sneezes, they say, *Alhamdulillah* (All praise and gratitude are for God) If another Muslim is nearby, he or she says, *Yarhamukallah* (God have mercy on you.) The recipient of this prayer then replies, *Yahdina wa yahdikumullah* (may God guide you and me to the right path).

Out of courtesy to those nearby, when one sneezes it is best to cover one's mouth, to try to limit the noise made, and to avoid spraying others by moving the head back and forth.[20]

Abu Hurayra said, "The Messenger of God told us, 'If your brother or sister (in faith) sneezes up to three times, say *yarhamukallah*. If they sneeze more than three times, they have a cold.'"[21] In another hadith Abu Hurayra again related, "God is pleased with sneezing, but displeased with yawning. Thus, if one of you sneezes and thanks God, other Muslims should say *yarhamukallah*. But yawning is from Satan. If one of you catches yourself yawning during the prayer, control yourself and do not make a yawning sound, for this is from Satan, who is making a mockery of you."[22]

In yet another hadith related by Abu Hurayra, "When God's Messenger sneezed, he would cover his face with his hands or garment and muffle the sound."[23]

Anas ibn Malik recalled, "Two people sneezed near the Prophet. He said *yarhamukallah* to one of them, but not the other one. When he was asked why, he said, 'This one thanked God, and that one did not.'"[24]

Abu Hurayra reports that the Prophet said, "Every Muslim has six rights over every other Muslim: When you meet each other, greet each other; when you are invited to someone's house, accept the invitation. If a Muslim asks advice from you, advise them. And if a Muslim sneezes and praises God, say *yarhamukallah* (God have mercy on you) in response. If they become ill, visit them; if they die, be willing to attend the funeral."[25]

ETIQUETTE OF ADVISING OTHERS
AND PUBLIC SPEAKING

One of the blessings of God Almighty to humankind is the ability to express our feelings and thoughts. As we learn in Sura Rahman, it was God Who taught us to speak; thus He created us with the natural ability to use words to express ourselves.

The Qur'an says, *"And say to My servants that they should always speak (even when disputing with others) that which is the best..."* (Isra 17:53), reminding us that good and kind words, as well as good counsel, can resolve hard feelings between hearts. In fact, when Moses and Aaron were sent to Pharaoh, God commanded them to *"speak to him with gentle words"* (TaHa 20:44).

From this perspective, even if we are speaking to someone who is an unbeliever, our religion directs us to approach them in a gentle manner. Again in the Qur'an God took a promise from the Children of Israel to *"speak kindly and well to people"* (Baqara 2:83). Today, when we are speaking with those who are different we should remember this Qur'anic command to speak gently and kindly. No matter who we are speaking to or what we are talking about, our manner of speech should be such that it will not put them off. The Messenger of God said, "A bad word will poison the entire discourse, making it appear ugly."[26]

Here follows a list of principles that need to be considered when speaking kindly and giving effective advice:

1. It is helpful if the addressee or audience can easily follow the line of thought in your talk, and pick out the main

ideas. Any kind of address can be made more effective by using clear transitions to signal the end of one point and the beginning of the next, and therefore listeners will know when the topic is changing. The main ideas should be pointed out at the beginning so that the audience can see where the speech or conversation is heading and how it is related to them.

2. If the audience cannot determine how the conversation or advice is applicable to them, the natural result is that they will lose interest in the subject. Therefore, when introducing a topic, one should state at the beginning how the advice can benefit those listening.

3. Ending a talk by saying something like "That is all I have to say" is unsatisfactory and reduces the effectiveness of the conversation or speech. The end of any speech is in fact more important than the introduction. To finish a talk in a compelling way one should reemphasize the purpose or main point of the speech, and the speaker should aim to inspire the listeners; after this the speaker should close by expressing pleasure for attention shown and thanking the listeners.

4. Advice should be clearly given and explained well; evidence should be provided for anything that others are to understand or accept.

5. Do not be afraid to speak the truth.

6. When addressing people, speaking about anything that is not useful knowledge concerned with religious or communal principles should be avoided. It should be obvious and clear to the audience, from the moment one begins to talk, what the subject is and what kind of things are going to be said about it.

7. Not even the smallest word, allusion or gesture that implies a form of ridicule or scorn should be included in any advice.

8. No matter what the topic of the advice or exhortation, the speaker will ultimately reveal something of their own personality. They should keep in mind that it is unfeasibly difficult to incite others to laudable actions without offering their sincere opinion on the issue. For advice to be effective, it is crucial that the speaker truly believes what they are saying; the audience should be able to perceive this belief. It is useless to try to make others believe what one does not believe oneself.

9. Keeping a serious tone and composure while speaking to an audience or giving advice is preferable.

THE RIGHTS OF NEIGHBORS

I n Islam neighborliness is very important. God commands us to treat all our neighbors well, whether or not we feel close to them:

> And (as the essential basis of contentment in individual, family and social life,) worship God and do not associate anything as a partner with Him; and do good to your parents in the best way possible, and to the relatives, orphans, the destitute, the neighbor who is near (in kinship, location, faith), the neighbor who is distant (in kinship and faith), the companion by your side (on the way, in the family, in the workplace, etc.), the wayfarer, and those who are in your service. (Treat them well and bring yourself up to this end, for) God does not love those who are conceited and boastful. (Nisa 4:36)

After our family, the people whose rights we should consider most are our neighbors; in Islam the rights of neighbors are strongly emphasized. We must get along well with our neighbors, as if they were part of our family circle, and help them when they are in need. After all, they are the people whose faces we see day after day, morning and night.

In a hadith recounted by Abu Hurayra, the Prophet said, "By God, that is not a believer!" and repeated this three times. They asked him, "Who do you mean, O Messenger?" and he answered, "He whose neighbor is not safe from him (is not a believer)!"[27]

In this hadith the phrase "is not a believer" means a person who is not a perfect, righteous believer. In other words, the Prophet was not categorically talking about a person who was not a Muslim. Therefore, in order to become a mature believer one must treat one's neighbors well. Another tradition related by Muslim says,

"One whose neighbors cannot be sure that he will not harm them cannot enter Heaven."[28]

The expression "cannot enter Heaven" probably is referring to people who do not go directly to Heaven. Thus, people who are not good neighbors will suffer the consequences of their actions, and only after that might they be admitted to Heaven.

God's Messenger said in another hadith, "Before buying a house look for a neighbor, and before setting out on a journey look for a friend."[29]

A Turkish proverb expresses this in another way: "Don't look at the house, look at the neighbor." The neighbor is far more important than the house. If one has bad neighbors, one cannot be comfortable or live in peace, even in the most beautiful house. For this reason the Prophet advised us to pray to God to save us from bad neighbors: "Always pray to God to protect you from bad neighbors where you dwell. (And remember that) your bad neighbors are temporary while moving from place to place."[30]

The religion of Islam teaches that neighbors do have rights over each other, and these are known, naturally enough, as "neighbor's rights." The following hadith from Aisha, the wife of the Prophet, demonstrates their great importance: "God's Messenger said, 'Gabriel emphasized the rights of neighbors to me so much that I thought he would give them inheritance rights.'"[31]

There is a meaningful example of this in Islamic history. Caliph Umar sent Muhammad ibn Maslama to Kufa to carry out an inspection for a construction site for Sa'd ibn Abi Waqqas, who was then the governor of Kufa, but he did not give him any provisions. After a nineteen-day journey Muhammad ibn Maslama returned to Medina; he then asked Umar why he had sent him without out provisions. Umar said, "The Muslims in Medina were on the verge of starving to death, so I did not want to be responsible for giving their provisions to you. I was there when God's Messenger said to us, "It is not fitting for a believer to have eaten his full when his neighbor is hungry."[32]

Thus we see that a person who knows that their neighbor is going to bed hungry but, despite this, does not help them cannot be a good Muslim.[33] At best, one who knowingly neglects to take care of their neighbors when they are in such a situation can be said to have a superficial faith. It must not be forgotten that the Prophet said, "Wherever someone goes hungry, that neighborhood will be far from God's protection."[34]

Helping neighbors is not a cause, but a result. The feeling and emotion of wanting to be helpful is the first step. Thus, it is essential to develop this desire in one's heart. Those who do not attempt to be as helpful as they can to those around them have not yet developed these sincere feelings. They cannot benefit from the pleasure of affection between neighbors.

Abu Dharr narrates, "God's Messenger recommended, 'When you prepare a broth, add extra water, and keep in mind the members of the household of your neighbors. Take some soup to those who need it; share your blessings.'"[35]

To offer food to one's neighbors is *Sunna*. A true Muslim will carefully honor the rights of their neighbors, show them a smiling face, lend to them if they need it, be there for them in trying times, and attempt to console them when they are in sorrow or grief. They will also avoid doing anything to annoy them, such as disturbing them with their waste. If a Muslim upsets their neighbors by making loud noise, like music or radios blaring from a window, without taking into consideration that their neighbor may be ill or trying to read, then they have neglected their neighbor's rights and ignored the duty that is owed to the community. Abu Hurayra tells how the Prophet once addressed this matter to his Companions:

"(One of the Companions) asked him, 'O Messenger of God! There is a woman who performs many supererogatory prayers, does extra fasting, and gives much in charity; but she offends her neighbors with her words.' The Prophet said, 'This woman is headed for Hell.' The Companion went on, 'O Messenger of God! There is a woman who does not do many supererogatory prayers or extra fasting, nor does she give much in charity; but she does not offend her neighbors with her words.' He said, 'This woman is headed for Heaven.'"

This clearly shows that people should work to gain the love and appreciation of their neighbors. Another hadith is also relevant:

One of the Companions came to God's Messenger and said, "'O God's Messenger! Tell me, what shall I do to get into Heaven?' Our Prophet considered the man's situation and gave him advice accordingly. According to Abu Hurayra another Companion came to ask a similar question, and the Prophet answered, "Be good." The Companion asked, "O Messenger! How shall I know if I am good?" He replied, "Ask your neighbors. If they think you are good, you are good; if they think you are bad, you are not a good person."[36]

This means that our neighbors—those closest to us, in one sense—know our good sides and bad sides. So if neighbors believe a person to be good, it is very likely that person is good in God's eyes too. But if neighbors believe someone to be bad, more than likely, they are bad in God's eyes.

Doubtless, there are also some applications of neighborliness that our children need to practice with neighbors. First of all, children should not take something they are about to eat, like a piece of fruit, outside. If there is a neighbor who cannot afford to buy such food, seeing it will make that person sad, because it will make their children sad. Children should accustom themselves to eating in the house, not out in the street, and remember that it is important to pay attention to this. In addition, this behavior will contribute to our children's development and understanding of general etiquette.

In his book *Marifetname*, Ibrahim Hakkı of Erzurum writes a list of "guidelines necessary for good neighborliness" that have been taken from Islamic teachings. Some of these are quoted here:

1. One's neighbors are not only those in adjoining houses, but everyone living nearby, up to forty doors away—in-

cluding non-Muslims. Treat them well, as if they were truly relatives.

2. Never go to bed full when a neighbor is hungry.
3. When cooking something that immediate neighbors can smell, take them some of it as a gift.
4. When a neighbor asks for a loan, give it.
5. On holidays, visit all neighbors.
6. Do not pry into the faults or secrets of neighbors.
7. Cover the faults of your neighbors.
8. Comfort your neighbors in hard times.
9. Visit your neighbor when they are unwell.
10. If a neighbor dies, try to go to his funeral.
11. If a neighbor child is orphaned, take the child in.[37]

VISITING FRIENDS

The religion of Islam teaches that all Muslims are brothers and sisters, and they should respect, help, and care for each other. One of the important ways to encourage the growth of such affection between people is to visit one another. In this respect Islam attaches great importance to visiting others for the sake of pleasing God. The Prophet said that a person who visits a sick person or a Muslim for the sake of God has a place prepared for them in Heaven.[38]

Visiting fosters feelings of caring, trust, unity, and togetherness in the community. Muslims get to know each other better through visiting. They can learn about one another's difficulties and problems. Visiting also provides an opportunity to give one another advice about various issues and to make decisions together. This helps people feel that they are not alone and to look towards the future with hope. When one is experiencing hardship or feeling down, seeing friendly faces helps one to feel more positive about life.

For a number of reasons today people live far from their parents; however, we are still responsible for visiting them whenever possible. A Muslim should visit their parents, relatives, neighbors, friends, and everyone they know, if possible. It is especially important on holidays. It is also appropriate at births, weddings, and deaths.

The following hadith speaks of the necessity of visiting neighbors and other friends. According to a narration by Qays ibn Sa'd, one of the Companions, God's Messenger came to visit him one day, stayed in his house for some time, prayed for him and then left his home. Another tradition recounts that the Prophet visited an Ansari family, ate a meal in their home, performed his *salat* (worship), and prayed for them while he was there.[39] 'Abdullah ibn

Qays also witnessed that "The Messenger would visit the Ansar, both individually and as a group. When he visited them individually, he went to their homes; when he wanted to see them as a group, he would go to the mosque."[40]

In light of the above narrations, it is clear that the Prophet visited Muslims often, and he always asked how they were doing. We can also see that the Prophet's Companions continued the practice of visiting each other, even when they lived in different regions. They would cross great distances to visit one another for the sake of God, even though traveling at that time incurred great difficulties. Salman, for instance, went from Midian to Damascus to see Abu al-Darda.[41] 'Abdullah ibn Mas'ud had the following conversation with his friends who came from Kufa to Medina to visit him: 'Abdullah asked, "Do you sit together and share your problems?" and his friends answered, "We have never neglected doing so." 'Abdullah then asked, "Do you visit one another?" The friends replied, "Yes, O Abu Abdur Rahman; in fact, if we have not seen some of our Muslim brothers for a long time, we walk all the way to the other end of Kufa to see them and to ask how they are." 'Abdullah replied, "As long as you continue to do this, you will live in peace."[42]

In order to visit people in the most appropriate manner there are some guidelines that should be followed. Under normal conditions, if these guidelines are not meticulously followed, a visit may not yield the expected benefits. Furthermore, to ignore the guidelines invites the risk of causing annoyance or difficulties for people instead of winning God's pleasure with the visit. The guidelines are:

1. A proper time should be selected for a visit. Normally, one should not visit during sleeping, eating, or working hours.

2. Clean, fresh clothing should be worn when making a visit, to avoid making the hosts uncomfortable.

3. If possible, one should give prior notice when planning to visit, including what time one is coming.

4. When visiting another's house, one should knock on the door, give salaams, inquire after the health of the inhabitants, and share good or bad events that have happened.

5. A visit should not be too long. The visitor should avoid saying anything hurtful or annoying, they should present a smiling, positive face with kind words, and try to share something that will please the host.

6. During visits, gossip and inappropriate topics should be avoided.

ASKING FOR PERMISSION

Asking permission from others is important as a general rule to be followed by both older and younger people and is emphasized in Islamic teachings. In fact such behavior is commanded in the verses of the Qur'an, which were revealed by God to be read century after century by each generation. Permission has a critical role in the life of both the family and society.

> O you who believe! Do not enter dwellings other than your own until you have ascertained the permission of their residents and have greeted them with peace. Your doing so is what is good and appropriate for you, so that you may be mindful (of good manners and proper courtesy). Then if you find no one in them, do not enter them until you have permission to enter. If you are asked to go back, then go back (without feeling offended). It is a purer way for you. God has full knowledge of all that you do. (Nur 24:27–28)

This Qur'anic verse emphasizes the sanctity and privacy of the home and lays out the rules that apply when visiting another person's home. Accordingly, if the visitor enters the home without waiting for the inhabitants to invite them in, they have shown a gross disregard for the privacy of the family. This verse, then, indicates that after knocking at the door or ringing the bell, a visitor should wait for permission to enter. Therefore, the best way to behave is first to greet the inhabitants of the house (or whoever comes to the door), saying *salaamun 'alaykum*, and then ask for permission to enter. In both the practice and teachings of Prophet Muhammad, peace and blessings be upon him, these guidelines can be seen in even greater detail. In fact, Imam Nawawi gave the following explanation: "God's Messenger said, 'First (utter) greetings, then anything else that needs to be said.' So the correct way is to greet people first and then ask (for permission) to enter." It is for this reason that great scholars like Abu Said al-Khudri raised their children to follow this rule of *adab*.

Ubayd ibn Umayr says, "Abu Musa al-Ash'ari came and asked to see Umar ibn Khattab. Umar must have been busy, and Abu Musa was not allowed in, so he left. When Umar finished what he was doing, he said, 'Did I hear the voice of Abu Musa? Let him in now!' When they told Umar that Abu Musa had left, he immediately had him called back. Then Umar asked him, 'Why didn't you wait?' Abu Musa replied, 'This is the way we were commanded to act.' Umar said, 'Bring me proof!' So Abu Musa went to the assembly of Ansar and asked them. They said, 'Only our youngest, Abu Said al-Khudri, can tell you firsthand about this matter.' So Abu Musa took Abu Said to Umar. When he heard what Abu Said had to say, Umar said, 'How can something that was taught and practiced by the Prophet have remained outside my knowledge? I must have been busy with trading or buying something at the market (when he taught that).'"

Caliph Umar was reminded of the rule that we should leave a place without becoming upset if permission is not granted by Abu Said al-Khudri, the child who had witnessed it in the life of the Prophet.[43]

The following tradition answers the most common questions about how waiting for permission is to be practiced. 'Abdullah ibn Busr recounted that the Prophet, when knocking on a door, would not look directly at the door, but turn his head to the side. If he was invited in, he would step in, if not he would turn back.[44] Islam forbids peeping into the houses of others, looking into them from the outside, or listening to conversations that take place in another's house. The Prophet stated that a person should ask for permission no more than three times. If there is no response, the would-be visitor should leave.

The Prophet, sent as a Mercy to the Worlds, would even ask for permission from children. Undoubtedly, he was the most righteous, the most trustworthy person in the whole world. Thus he made no distinction between younger and older people (but observed their rights equally). Sahl ibn Sa'd says, "(Once I saw) someone bring a drink to the Prophet. He drank from it, then he turned to the child on his right. There were some older people on his left. He asked the child, 'Do you mind if I give them some of this?' The child said, 'No, by God; O Messenger, I do not wish for you to give to anyone else what you give to me!' And the Prophet gave the child the water."[45]

ACCEPTING INVITATIONS

The Qur'an says,

> O you who believe! Do not enter the Prophet's rooms (in his house) unless you are given leave, (and when invited) to a meal, without waiting for the proper time (when the meal is to be served). Rather, when you are invited, enter (his private rooms) at the proper time; and when you have had your meal, disperse. Do not linger for mere talk. That causes trouble for the Prophet, and he is shy of (asking) you (to leave). But God does not shy away from (teaching you) the truth...." (Ahzab 33:53)

There are two basic elements that are important among the many aspects present in this verse. They are:

1. Waiting to be invited before joining a meal;
2. After enjoying a meal as a guest, not overstaying one's welcome or talking too much.

The revelation of this verse was occasioned by some people who would come to the Prophet's house unannounced at odd hours and stay, not wanting to leave until they had been served a meal. But clearly this is a general Islamic principle that is applicable to anyone who is a guest at someone else's home. Therefore, it is clear that one must not "invite oneself" or join a dinner or gathering without being invited. One day Abu Shuayb saw the Messenger of God among his Companions and understood from his face that he was hungry. He immediately said to his kitchen help, "Prepare a meal for five people, with me as the fifth. I want to invite God's Messenger tonight." Then he went over to the Prophet and extended the invitation. They walked back to his house together, but another man from the group followed them. When they reached Abu Shuayb's door, the Prophet said, "This man has followed me here. If you want, accept him; if you want, send him back." Abu Shuayb said, "No, O God's Messenger; he can join us too."[46]

In this hadith, if one looks closely, the Prophet was exercising Islamic *adab*. It is certain that believers take pleasure in hosting each other. But there are certain guidelines and boundaries that come with invitations and visits. An unannounced visitor can cause a host to worry, "What should I serve?" If they do not have much, this can in turn create financial hardship for them. At the same time, when a brother or sister in faith extends an invitation to a fellow Muslim for a meal or a visit, it should be accepted, as this will foster affection and closeness between them. This is stated in the hadith, "When you are invited, accept the invitation." Nafi also said, "Ibn Umar accepted invitations to weddings and other invitations, even when he was fasting."[47] When one is invited, it is not good manners to reject or to avoid acceptance. The following hadith shows that not accepting invitations and showing up somewhere without being invited are both examples of poor manners: "He who does not accept an invitation which he receives has disobeyed God and His Messenger. And he who enters without invitation enters as a thief and goes out as a plunderer."[48]

What if one is invited somewhere by two different people on the same day or at the same time? This is also addressed in Islam: Humayd ibn Abdir Rahman al-Himyari heard the Messenger say, "If two people invite you at the same time, accept the invitation of the one whose door is closest to yours, for this is the closer neighbor. But if one invited you first, accept the first invitation."[49] Another thing that close attention should be paid to is that forbidden foods or drinks should not be consumed when one is invited out. A Muslim should not even go to places where forbidden things are done unless they can put a stop to the forbidden behaviors or if the others cease doing it in their presence out of respect.

For the host, it is important that no one is brought to the gathering who will upset the other guests. When the guests get up to leave, the host should ask them to stay a little longer, without insisting too much. Gatherings should also be kept simple and not extravagant. When we are about to eat, if there are friends or relatives around who know we are eating, good *adab* requires asking them to join us.

It is also good *adab* to share with the person who delivers or brings the food we eat, as this narration shows: Anas (who worked in the Prophet's household) said, "Umm Sulaym sent me to God's Messenger with a basket of dates. But I found God's Messenger out. Just before I came, he had left to accept the invitation of a former slave who had now been freed. So I immediately went there. When I arrived, they were eating. They invited me to eat with them. The host had made a dish of broth with pumpkin and sop. I saw that God's Messenger liked the pumpkin, so I put pieces of pumpkin before him, (so that he could eat what was next to him). After we ate, he got up and went back home. Then, I handed him the basket of dates from Umm Sulaym, and he offered dates to everyone there, including me. We finished the dates together."[50]

BEING CLEAN AND POLITE
AT GATHERINGS

I t is clearly of great importance to be clean when going some-where where other people will be. In addition, scholars and elders should be seated in the places of honor. It is good manners to listen at gatherings or meetings and not to speak un-necessarily. Also, we should make room for those who arrive later and greet them with a smile. It is not proper to stand up for those who arrive. There was no one more beloved to the Companions than the Prophet. Despite this, they did not stand up when he ar-rived, for they knew he did not like this behavior.[51] As told by Abu Umama, one day the Messenger came to them walking with a staff. When the Companions stood up, he said, "Do not stand up as others do to flatter one another!"[52] Another occurrence also demonstrates this well:

One time Muawiya came to see Ibn al-Zubayr and Ibn Amr. Ibn Amr stood up, but Ibn al-Zubayr stayed sitting (did not stand). Muawiya said to Ibn Amr, "Sit down, for God's Messenger said, 'Those who are pleased when people stand up for them should pre-pare their place in the fire.'"[53]

It is not appropriate to sit between two people who do not want to be separated. The Messenger commanded, "It is not per-missible to sit between two people without their permission." In a narration of Tirmidhi, the same idea is expressed: "It is forbidden for a person to come between two other people without their permission."[54]

It is also improper for two people in a group of three to put their heads together and whisper. This could make the third person sad and lead to doubt. The Messenger said, "When you are three people together, two of you should not speak of something between you; this will make the other person upset."[55] If you need to discuss something with a person the correct thing to do is to take leave of the other friends and go somewhere else. If someone leaves a gathering temporarily it is not right to immediately occupy their place. When a person left their seat, 'Abdullah ibn Umar—one of the Companions—would never sit there.[56] The Messenger taught us, "If someone leaves for some reason and comes back again, they have the right to sit in the same place."[57]

VISITING THE SICK

M uslims should visit their sick friends and neighbors at an appropriate time, and also pray for their health. This is not only a duty, but a way to strengthen the bonds of affection between them.

It is *Sunna* to visit those who are ill. Prophet Muhammad, peace and blessings be upon him, visited sick people and encouraged believers to do the same.[58] When we visit a believer who is unwell, we can boost their morale and also gain rewards for this good action.[59]

It is difficult to fully appreciate the value of health until one becomes ill. Illness is a trial that requires submission to God's will, and reliance on His care. The Prophet said that to visit invalids and attend funerals is a reminder of the Hereafter.[60] When he visited someone who was unwell, he would put his hand on their forehead, take their hand, ask how they were feeling, and pray for them, saying, "May you get well; may your illness purify you from sins."[61]

In a *hadith qudsi* God's Messenger said, "God will say on the Judgment Day, 'My servant was ill and you did not visit him (her); if you had, you would have found Me there.'"[62] His wife Aisha reported that when a member of his own family became ill, the Prophet would pray for them thus: "O God, the Lord and Sustainer of all people! Make this pain pass. You are the Healer; none can heal except You."[63] He directed Muslims who were unwell to "put your hand on the part of your body that is in pain, say *Bismillah* (In the Name of God) thrice, and then repeat seven times, 'I take refuge in God Almighty from the harm and danger of my illness.'"[64] He also advised, "If someone is on their deathbed, recommend that they recite the *shahada* of *La ilaha illallah Muhammadan rasulullah*, which means, "There is no deity other than God, and Muhammad is the Messenger of God."

God's Messenger visited people who were ill regardless of whether or not they were Muslim.[65] It is a duty for Muslims to visit those who are not well. When you are with a sick person, always speak positively and boost their morale. The Prophet said the following about visiting believers who are unwell: "The believers are as one body, one in love, mercy, and compassion. Whenever any organ or limb of the body is unwell, the other parts also feel pain."[66]

Prophet Muhammad, peace and blessings be upon him, spread the best morals and created an environment of mutual assistance and brotherhood, which was ornamented with the highest altruistic emotions. Visiting the ill is one of these humane values, as this makes those who are unwell feel less alone and less helpless in the face of mortality; it lightens their burden and lessens the chances that they may fall into despair or misery. Everyone, even members of another religion, should be visited when they fall ill, as the Messenger visited people who were unwell, regardless of their religion. There is a hadith related by Anas ibn Malik that says, "There was a non-Muslim serving God's Messenger. One day he became ill. The Prophet went to visit him and sat by his bed. He asked the man to become a Muslim. The servant looked at his father, who was also at his side. His father said, 'Obey Abu al-Qasim (the Prophet).' And this man became Muslim. When God's Messenger was leaving the place he said, 'Praise be to God, Who has saved him from the fire.'"[67]

When one is ill, one must not show impatience with the illness or with one's visitors. To cry and complain or to wail, or to wish for death are not honorable actions. The Prophet once said, "Do not wish for death because of a trial that befalls you. If one of you truly wishes to die, let him say, 'My God, if life is better for me, let me live; if death is better for me, then let me die.'"[68]

There is no obstacle to prevent a man visiting a woman who is ill if he observes the proper formalities.[69] In fact, visiting the ill is so important that a believer should even visit a sinful Muslim if they are sick. The purpose of a visit is to make the ill person feel less alone, to raise their morale and hope, and to cheer them. Serious illnesses brings death to people's minds, and therefore it is advisable to say to people that we will all return to God, that every person's appointed hour will come, and that nothing can cause a person to die before or after the destined hour.[70] It is also a good idea to bring gifts to people who are unwell.[71] But we should not forget to ask how the person is doing; to fail to do so means that we have not followed the Prophet's example.[72]

The Prophet once visited a sick Muslim and prayed the following prayer for them: "O God, give us good in all things in this world, give us uncountable blessings in the Hereafter, and save us from the fire of Hell."[73]

FUNERAL ETIQUETTE

It is a Muslim's duty to another Muslim who has died to go to their funeral, to stay until they have been covered with earth, and to pray for that they will be forgiven. In a hadith God's Messenger said, "Whoever attends a funeral until the prayers are finished receives one *carat* of reward. Whoever stays at a funeral until the dead person is buried earns two *carats* of reward. And a *carat* is like the size of Mount Uhud."[74]

The purpose of attending funerals is both to do our duty by our brothers and sisters in faith, by burying them, and also to be reminded of death by seeing the graves of others.

The Prophet taught us, "Do not follow a funeral (procession) with noisy laments or with fire." Another narration adds, "Do not walk in front of a funeral procession."[75] He also taught that it was necessary to think of death often, which "sours worldly pleasures." In Islam this meditation on death means that each person should consider that they will not be benefited by anything—family, friends, or possessions—when they draw their final breath; with the expiration of that breath, the body and all its organs will be left behind by the spirit.

In several different places in the Qur'an we are told, *"Every human being is bound to taste death."*[76] In addition to these, other verses point out that no person will remain in this world forever,[77] that people come into the world to be tested,[78] and that fleeing from death will not profit anyone.[79] Furthermore, we are told that everyone will return to God[80] and that the purpose of life is to remember and mention God much, reflecting on the blessings God provides.[81]

According to *Sunna* four people carry the coffin on four sides. The Prophet instructed, "Whoever goes to a funeral and takes three turns bearing the remains (to the grave), has completed his duty to his brother/sister (in faith)."[82] It is better for those who follow a funeral procession to walk behind the pallbearers. However, it is not reprehensible to walk in front of the coffin, as this is what God's Messenger, Abu Bakr, Umar, and Uthman did.[83]

When following a funeral procession, we should meditate on the end of our lives, as is appropriate for the occasion, and take this as a serious lesson. It is unseemly to talk and laugh or be preoccupied with trivial worldly matters in such circumstances. Even to recite the Qur'an or prayers in a loud voice is discouraged, as loud noise should be avoided, including weeping. Those in the procession should try to prevent such acts. Anyone who has started out in the procession should continue to the end, barring an emergency.

Naturally, there is no reason one should not weep for grief. It is simply best to avoid unnecessary words or excessive wailing, and to remember that God is ultimately the Giver of Life and the Dealer of Death.

The Prophet said in a hadith, "Speak well of the dead; do not mention their faults."[84] On another occasion, a funeral procession passed by the Prophet. The people were speaking of the good qualities of the person who had died. He said thrice, "It is so!" Then another funeral procession passed. The people then said how bad the dead person had been. And the Prophet said again, "It is so!" When they asked him, "O Messenger of God! What is so?" he answered, "The first person had good things said about him; for him Heaven is waiting. But they had bad things to say about the second person; for him Hell is waiting, (for) you are God's witnesses on the face of the earth."[85]

VISITING GRAVES

God's Messenger encouraged the visiting of graveyards as it reminds Muslims of life in the Hereafter. The Prophet said, "Mention death often, for it shatters pleasure."[86] Another hadith says, "Visiting tombs was forbidden before, but now it should be done, for the dead will remind you of the next life."[87] Imam Abu Hanifa said to Imam Abu Yusuf, "If you have benefited from someone's knowledge or the wisdom of some scholar, pray to God to forgive them, read the Qur'an, and visit their tombs."

The legitimacy, as well as the benefits, of visiting graves is shown in these narrations. However, there are also some guidelines about how graves should be visited. During such visits, no requests or help should be asked of the dead. It is stated in the first chapter of the Qur'an, "*Only You do we worship, and only You do we ask for help.*" This verse clearly means that worship is only for God and help is only from God. It is clear that it is incompatible with the Islamic faith to ask of dead people favors that only God can grant.

When visiting graves, it is proper to greet the dead souls, "O inhabitants of the land of the dead! God's peace be upon you. God willing, one day we will meet again." Then we should recite the Qur'an and pray for the forgiveness of the departed souls. There is no definite day set aside for visiting graves, but Fridays or Saturdays, as well as holidays and the day before the Eids are good times for such visits. Indeed, it is recorded in the hadith that the Prophet visited graves on such days.

The hadith I have chosen to include regarding the benefits of recitation of the Qur'an or giving charity for the departed will, I believe, serve to clarify this issue. Ibn Abbas related, "The mother of

Sa'd ibn Ubada passed away. He came to the Prophet and asked, 'O Messenger of God! My mother died while I was away from her. If I give charity in her name will it benefit her?' The Messenger replied, 'Yes.' Then Sa'd asked, 'O Prophet! Be my witness; I give my fruit garden as charity in my mother's name.'"[88]

The Prophet also advised, "When a person dies, their book of deeds is closed. Only three things are exceptions: the benefits of their charity, the knowledge they have shared, and surviving children who pray for them."[89]

These hadith teach that for believers who have passed away the good they did in life continues to bring them blessings after death; it also urges their relatives and fellow believers to continue to pray for them since this will also benefit them.

The benefits and lessons of visiting graves can be put in order of priority thus:

1. Visiting the graves reminds people of death and the Hereafter, motivating them to prepare themselves for the next life.

2. It develops God-consciousness. It discourages people from committing prohibited acts, and from greed, and encourages them to do good.[90]

3. Visiting the resting places of the Prophet and other holy people provides relief to souls and fosters higher emotions. Traveling to see the graves of the Prophet and others of God's servants is a commendable act. In fact, the Prophet said in a hadith, "Whoever visits me after I die it will be as if they have visited me during my lifetime."[91]

4. To visit tombs reminds people of history, as well as helping to strengthen their understanding of history and the religious background of their people.

GOOD WILL AND HELPING OTHERS

Muslims want the best for everyone, and feel pleasure in helping others. To help one another and intercede for one another is one of the directives of Islam and to do so is demanded by the brotherhood that exists between Muslims. One who wants something good for themselves but does not want the same thing for others has violated the basic social principles of Islam.

What the right thing to do is, or its manner and method, can change according to the circumstances and the environment. It is not always necessary to be direct. When practicing the feelings of goodness and mercy, there are certainly motifs that need to be attended to. These are sensitivity of heart, sincerity, loving goodness, and the desire to seek God's pleasure. Also important are concerns like avoiding the expectation of repayment, looking for thanks, or pursuing worldly profit and advantage. There is also a faith dimension to helpfulness and the desire to work for the comfort and peace of others. One of the sayings of the Prophet is, "If one of you does not want or love for his brother (or neighbor) what he wants and loves for himself, he cannot be a true believer."

It is important to be resolute in the gaining of God's pleasure, to be full of merciful feelings toward the needy, and to be ready to put others before oneself, helping them with their problems whenever necessary. It will certainly benefit us if we try to complete our duties of helping others, constantly seeking opportunities to please God, and taking shelter in God's mercy. People who practice such behavior will be given rewards *like no eye has seen, no ear has heard, and no human mind can possibly imagine*" in Paradise.

According to a narration by Abu Hurayra, God's Messenger said, "All people owe a debt of gratitude to God in return for the benefit of every limb and joint of their body every day, and their giving thanks or acknowledging all these blessings is an important *sadaqa* (charity). For example, it is *sadaqa* to make peace between two who are fighting. It is also a great *sadaqa* to help someone to climb onto their animal or to lift their load. A good word is also a *sadaqa*. Every step taken to get to prayers (for any *salat* such as congregational prayers, funeral prayers, Eid prayers) is *sadaqa*. The removal of a harmful object from the road so it will not bother others is even accepted as *sadaqa*."[92] Having been granted such blessings, the *sadaqa* that we owe is to use them to work for good. The debt of gratitude owed for such blessings is a key to understanding some essential aspects of social *adab*. For example, every step a person takes to get to prayers is counted as *sadaqa*, resulting in the forgiveness of a sin and raising the person's degree.

MOSQUE ETIQUETTE

When someone enters a mosque, the "House of God (i.e., a building that has been appointed for the worship of God)," they should ensure that they are physically and ritually clean. This is why ritual purification from a state of major ritual impurity is necessary for those in this state before they enter a mosque. The most common causes of major ritual impurity are associated with seminal emission, intercourse, menses, or childbirth. (However, according to the Hanafi and Maliki schools, one in this state may enter if necessary by performing *tayammum*, or dry ablution, with clean earth where there is no water available. Also, if the person is not going to stay in the mosque but only stop there briefly on a journey, the Shaafi and Hanbali schools allow them to enter.) According to the Hanbali, it is permissible for someone in a state of major ritual impurity to enter the mosque after having ablution and without *ghusl*, or full washing of the body with water. So that everyone can come, whether or not they are ritually clean or in a state to be able to perform *salat* (for example, women in their menses), Eid prayers and funerals are generally held outside the mosque at a different location. Further, it is permissible, but discouraged, to enter the mosque without taking ablution. It is disrespectful to use a mosque with two doors simply as a path (i.e., to go through it on one's way somewhere else).

There are some short prayers the Prophet used to recite when entering a mosque which are mentioned in the hadith. In one such narration, the Prophet entered a mosque, uttered the greeting of peace, and then prayed, "My God, open the doors of Your mercy to me!" When he left, he again gave the peace greeting and prayed,

"My God, I hope for Your beneficence and kindness!" He also used to enter the mosque by stepping in first with his right foot and leave it with his left foot.

Once the *adhan*, or call to prayer, has been called, no one who is inside the mosque (who is in a fit state for *salat*) should get up and leave without performing the *salat* with the others. When entering the mosque, one should be considerate of anything that could make others uncomfortable or distract them. The Prophet asked people, for instance, not to come to the mosque after eating strong-smelling foods like garlic. He also forbade people from making too much noise in the mosque. Once, when someone disturbed the congregation by looking for something he had lost, the Prophet said, "Let it not be found!" The atmosphere in the mosque should be peaceful because this is a place devoted to worship. In addition to the above-mentioned items, people should also be careful not to pass in front of someone who is performing *salat*, brush against others or push their way in front of others (in crowded congregations).

When it comes to young children or others (such as the mentally disabled) who cannot understand the etiquette of entering a mosque, it is not advised to bring them to the mosque. When children reach the age of reason, it is a good idea to take them to the mosque and accustom them to congregational prayers, and also teach them to read and recite the Qur'an in the mosque.

It is discouraged, even prohibited according to some schools of thought, to sell, buy, or hire out things, or carry out any transactions for profit in a mosque; however, raising donations is acceptable. There are scholars who say that it is not permissible to beg or give to beggars in the mosque, but charity can be given to those who need it if they have not asked for it. Inside the mosque speaking is allowed as long as one does not make other people uncomfortable. At the same time, it is not proper to go to the mosque solely to chat, nor to speak too loudly, or even to pray so loudly that it bothers others. In order to avoid dirtying the mosque, people should not sleep or eat there, with some exceptions in the Hanafi and Maliki schools, including circumstances such as putting up guests or traveling.

It is recommended that the mosque be closed between prayer times if common sense dictates that to do so is safer for whatever items are found inside; however, if there is no need to secure the property, it is better not to close the mosque. Abu Hanifa and Imam Malik were of the opinion that the funeral prayer should be performed outside the mosque, except in the case of inclement weather. However, for Shaafis and Hanbalis there is no such preference.

CONCLUSION

In this work we have tried to address some of the ethical concepts, guidelines for morality, and religious teachings which have formed Islamic culture and which I believe to be indispensable for daily life. All the subjects that I have chosen to focus on are much more valuable and useful when put into practice, rather than simply recognized.

It also makes sense that these precepts of religion and morality are approached as Divine directives, since every topic touched upon is taken either from Qur'anic verses or Prophetic traditions.

These moral principles are the source of many types of virtues and much good. If they are truly practiced and lived, not just outwardly, then they can lead to the development of a moral character that brings harmony between the spiritual and the physical, the outward and the inward. Thus, a new generation possessing the finest character will arise and in the end they will bring light to the community with their excellent morals and ethics.

I wish health and inner peace to you and to all humankind.

NOTES

CHAPTER 1: CHARACTER AND ETHICS

1 Muslim, *Birr*, 15, Hadith 2553; Tirmidhi, *Zuhd*, 52, Hadith 2390.

2 Tirmidhi, *Birr* 77, Hadith 2019.

3 Muslim, *Birr*, 33; Ibn Maja, *Zuhd*, 9; Ibn Hanbal, *Musnad*, 2/285, 539.

4 Ajluni, *Kashf al-Khafa*, I, 425.

5 Muslim, *Qadar*, 34.

6 Tirmidhi, *Rida*, 11, Hadith 1162; Abu Dawud, *Sunna*, 16, Hadith 4682.

7 *Akhtar al-Kabir,* see the entry for "*alif-dal*".

8 *Lisan al-Arab*, see the entry for "*adb*".

9 *T.D.V. İslam Ansiklopedisi*, (Encyclopedia of Islam) Vol. 10, 412.

10 Ibn Hajar, *Fath al-Bari*, 13/2.

11 Ajluni, *Kashf al-Khafa*, 1/70.

12 *T.D.V. İslam Ansiklopedisi*, (Encyclopedia of Islam) Vol. 10, 412.

13 Muwatta, *Husn al-Khulq*, 8; Ibn Hanbal, *Musnad*, 2/381.

14 Tirmidhi, *Birr*, 41, Hadith 1963.

15 Muwatta, *Husn al-Khulq*, 1.

16 Tirmidhi, *Birr*, 62, Abu Dawud, *Adab*, 8, Hadith 4799.

17 Nasai, *Iftitah*, 16.

18 Tirmidhi, *Birr*, 62, Hadith 2001.

19 Yazir, *Hak Dini Kur'an Dili* (The Qur'an, the Language of the True Religion), p. 4479.

20 Ibn Kathir, *Tafsir*, Muhtasar, 3/667.

21 Suyuti, *Jami al-Saghir*, 3/3416.

22 Tirmidhi, *Birr*, 62, 2003–2004; Abu Dawud, *Adab* 8, 4799.

23 Nawawi, *Riyad al-Salihin*, Vol. 1, 49–54.

24 See Bukhari, *Adab*; Muslim, *Adab*, Muwatta, *Khulq*

25 Muslim, *Qadar*, 25.

26 Muslim, *Qadar*, 22.

27 *Akhtar al-Kabir*, the entry for "*ayn-shin*".

CHAPTER 2: GOOD EDUCATION AND UPBRINGING

1 Ibn Maja, *Muqaddima*, 16.

2 Bukhari, *Ilm*, 13; *I'tisam*, 10; Muslim, *Imarat*, 98, 1038; *Zakat*, 98, 100, Tirmidhi, *Ilm*, 1, 2647.

3 Abu Dawud, *Ilm*, 9, 3658; Tirmidhi, *Ilm*, 3, 2651.

4 Abu Dawud, *Ilm*, 10, 3661; Bukhari, *Ashab al-Nabi*, 9; Muslim, *Fadail al-Ashab*, 34, 2046.

5 Tirmidhi, *Ilm*, 19, 2684.

6 Bukhari, *Daawat*, 20.

7 Bukhari, *Ilm*, 49.

8 Muslim, *Muqaddima*, 5.

9 Bukhari, *Ilm*, 10; Abu Dawud, *Ilm*, 1; Tirmidhi, *Ilm*, 19; Ibn Maja, *Muqaddima*, 17.

10 Haysami, *Majma al-Zawaid wa Manba al-Fawaid*, Vol. 1, pp. 123–124.

11 Ibn Maja, *Muqaddima*, 23.

12 Bukhari, *Ilm*, 15.

13 Ibn Maja, *Muqaddima*, 17.

14 Tirmidhi, *Ilm*, 19.

15 Ghazali, *Ihya al-Ulum al-Din*, 1/7.

16 Haysami, *Majma al-Zawaid wa Manba al-Fawaid*, Vol. 1, p. 122.

17 Ghazali, *Ihya al-Ulum al-Din*, 1/11.

18 Tirmidhi, *Birr*, 73; Ibn Hanbal, *Musnad*, 5/323.

19 Tirmidhi, *Kutub al-Sitta* (Abridged), 16/550.

20 Abdul Fattah Abu Ghudda, *Safahat Min Sabr al-Ulama*, 37.

21 Sam'ani, *Adab al-Imla wa al-Istimla*, 36.

22 Bukhari, *Salat*, 106; *Adab*, 18; Muslim, *Masajid*, 41/5, 43; Muwatta, *Kasr al-Salat*, 81/1, 170; Abu Dawud, *Salat*, 169/917–920; Nasai, *Masajid*, 19/2,45; *Sahw*, 13/3, 10.

23 Bukhari, *Adhan*, 65; Muslim, *Salat*, 189/469–470; 196/473; Tirmidhi, *Salat*, 175/237, 276; Nasai, *Imamat*, 35/2, 94–94.

24 Nasai, *Iftitah*, 83/2, 229–230.

25 Abu Dawud, *Sawm*, 43, 2408; Tirmidhi, *Sawm*, 21, 715; Nasai, *Sawm*, 51/4, 180–182; Ibn Maja, *Siyam*, 12, 1668.

26 Bukhari, *Talaq*, 11.

27 Bukhari, *Shahada*, 18; *Maghazi*, 29; Muslim, *Imara*, 91, 1868; Tirmidhi, *Jihad*, 31, 1711; Abu Dawud, *Hudud*, 17; 4406–7; Nasai, *Talaq*, 20/6, 155.

28 Abu Dawud, *Salat*, 362, 1532.

29 Ibn Hanbal, *Musnad*, 3/435.

30 Bukhari, *Adab*, 18; Muslim, *Fadail*, 65.

31 Bukhari, *Tajrid al-Sarih*, 12/152.

32 Muslim, *Fadail*, 51.

33 Abu Dawud, *Adab*, 20.

34 Bukhari, *Jizya*, 12; *Diyat*, 22; Nasai, *Kasama*, 4.

35 Tirmidhi, *Jihad*, 24; Abu Dawud, *Jihad*, 70.

36 Tirmidhi, *Birr*, 15; Abu Dawud, *Adab*, 58.

37 Ibid.

38 Abu Dawud, *Adab*, 23.

39 Munawi, *Fayd al-Kadir*, 3/220.

40 Ajluni, *Kashf al-Khafa*, 2/230.

41 Abu Dawud, *Adab*, 5223.

42 Haysami, *Majma al-Zawaid*, 8/15.

43 Tirmidhi, *Sunan, Tafsir of Sura Isra*, Ibn Maja, *Sunan*, 2/1221.

44 *Musafaha* is dealt with in detail in chapter 4.

45 Bukhari, *Hiba*, 28; *Adab*, 8; Muslim, *Zakat*, 50, 1003; Abu Dawud, *Zakat*, 34, 1668.

46 Munawi, *Fayz al-Qadir*, 5/483.

47 Haysami, *Majma al-Zawaid*, 8/156.

48 Tirmidhi, *Birr*, 3, 1901.

49 Tirmidhi, *Birr*, 3, 1900.

50 Abu Dawud, *Adab*, 129, 5142; Ibn Maja, *Adab*, 2, 3664.

51 Muslim, *Birr*, 9, 251; Tirmidhi, *Daawat*, 110, 3539.

52 Bukhari, *Zakat*, 1.

53 Ibn Hanbal, *Musnad*, 2/484.

54 Bukhari, *Ilm*, 37; Muslim, *Iman*, 74–77.

55 Muslim, *Birr wa Sila* 17.

56 Bukhari, *Adab*, 11.

57 Bukhari, *Adab*, 12.

58 Tirmidhi, *Zakat*, 26.

59 Tirmidhi, *Birr*, 5.

60 Bukhari, *Adab*, 15.

61 Bukhari, *Adab*, 4; Muslim, *Iman*, 146, 90; Tirmidhi, *Birr*, 4, 1903; Abu Dawud, *Adab*, 129, 5141.

62 Tirmidhi, *Da'wat*, 100, 3525.

63 Bukhari, *Jum'a*, 8/2, 212; *Wudu*, 73; *Tahajjud*, 9; Muslim, *Tahara*, 45, 254; Abu Dawud, *Tahara*, 30, 55; Nasai, *Tahara*, 2/1, 8.

64 Abu Dawud, *Tahara*, 27, 30/51, 56–7; Muslim, *Tahara*, 45, 253; Nasai, *Tahara*, 8/1, 13.

65 Tirmidhi, *Da'wat*, 112, 3543–4.

66 Abu Dawud, *Salat*, 307, 1308; Nasai, *Kiyam al-Layl*, 5/3, 205.

67 Muslim, *Musafirin*, 162, 755; Tirmidhi, *Salat*, 334, 465.

68 Tirmidhi, *Da'wat*, 96, 3518.

69 Bukhari, *Fadail al-Qur'an*, 14; *Tibb*, 39; *Da'wat*, 12; Muslim, *Salam*, 50, 2192; Muwatta, *'Ayn*, 15/2, 942; Tirmidhi, *Da'wat*, 21, 3399; Abu Dawud, *Tibb*, 19, 3902.

70 Tirmidhi, *Da'wat*, 34.

71 Yazir, *Hak Dini Kur'an Dili*, IX.

72 Muslim, *Tahara*, 1; Tirmidhi, *Da'wat*, 86; Ibn Hanbal, *Musnad*, 4/260, 5/432–4, 363, 370, 372; Darimi, *Wudu*, 2.

73 Tirmidhi, *Adab*, 41.

74 Muslim, *Tahara*, 68; Abu Dawud, *Tahara*, 15; Ibn Hanbal, *Musnad*, 2/372.

75 Muslim, *Tahara*, 20–1, 237.

76 Abu Dawud, *Tahara*, 27, 30 (51, 56–7); Muslim, *Tahara*, 45/253; Nasai, *Tahara*, 8/1, 3.

77 Nasai, *Tahara*, 5/ 1, 10.

78 Bukhari, *Wudu*, 26; Muslim, *Tahara*, 87/278; Muwatta, *Tahara*, 9/1, 21; Abu Dawud, *Tahara*, 49/103–5; Tirmidhi, *Tahara*, 19/24; Nasai, *Tahara*, 1/1, 6–7.

79 Tirmidhi, *Tahara*, 40/53.

80 Nasai, *Ziynat*, 83/ 8, 196; Tirmidhi, *Birr*, 63, 2007.

81 Abu Dawud, *Libas*, 8, 4037.

82 Tirmidhi, *Da'wat*, 119, 3555; Ibn Maja, *Libas*, 2, 3557.

83 Abu Dawud, *Libas*, 14, 4057; Nasai, *Ziynat*, 40/8, 160.

84 Abu Dawud, *Tarajjul*, 1552.

85 Abu Dawud, *Tarajjul*, 14.

86 Bukhari, *Libas,* 72; Muslim, *Libas,* 72; Abu Dawud, *Tarajjul*, 14; Nasai, *Ziynat,* 5; Ibn Maja, *Libas,* 38; Ibn Hanbal, *Musnad*, 2, 39. This hadith was also reported by Abu Hanifa. See Zabidi, *Uqud al-Jawahir al-Munifa*, 2, 156.

87 Abu Dawud, *Tarajjul*, 13; Nasai, *Ziynat,* 57; Ibn Hanbal, *Musnad*, 1, 204.

88 Abu Dawud, *Libas*, 4; Ibn Hanbal, *Musnad*, 2, 50.

89 Hakim al-Nisaburi, *Mustadrak*, 4, 150.

90 Gülen, *Prizma*, IV, 119–123.

CHAPTER 3: WHAT GOOD CHARACTER REQUIRES

1 Mawlana Shibli, *Asr al-Saada*, 2/108.

2 Muslim, *Jihad*, Hadith 3357.

3 Bukhari, *Tibb*, 47, 49–50, *Jizya*, 14, *Adab*, 56; Muslim, *Salam*, 43, 2189.

4 Ibn Sa'd, *Tabaqat*, Vol. 1, 360.

5 Bukhari, *Khumus*, 16; Muslim, *Zakat*, 142, 1063.
6 Bukhari, *Wudu*, 58; Abu Dawud, *Tahara*, 138/380; Tirmidhi, *Tahara*, 112/147; Nasai, *Tahara*, 45/1, 48–49.
7 Bukhari, *Libas*, 18, *Khumus*, 19, *Adab*, 68.
8 Bukhari, *Adab*, 39; Muslim, *Fadail*, 13; Tirmidhi, *Birr*, 69.
9 Azimabadi, *Awn al-Ma'bud*, 127.
10 Muslim, *Birr*, 78, 2594; Abu Dawud, *Jihad*, 1, 2578, *Adab*, 11, 4808.
11 Muslim, *Birr*, 106, 2608; Abu Dawud, *Adab*, 3, 4779.
12 Muslim, *Birr*, 75, 2592.
13 Bukhari, *Adab*, 76; Tirmidhi, *Birr*, 73, 2021; Muwatta, *Husn al-Khulq*, 11/2, 96.
14 Abu Dawud, *Adab*, 4, 4784.
15 Abu Dawud, *Adab*, 4, 4782.
16 Tirmidhi, *Ilm*, 16.
17 Tirmidhi, *Fitan*, 26, 2191.
18 Tirmidhi, *Dawat*, 53, 3448; Abu Dawud, *Adab*, 4, 4780.
19 Bukhari, *Adab*, 76; Tirmidhi, *Birr*, 73, 2021; Muwatta, *Husn al-Khulq*, 11/2, 906.
20 Bukhari, *I'tisam*, 2; Tafsir, *A'raf*, 5.
21 Bukhari, *Ahqam*, 13; Muslim, *Aqdiya*, 16, 1717; Tirmidhi, *Ahqam*, 7, 1334; Abu Dawud, *Aqdiya*, 9, 3589; Nasai, *Qudat*, 17/8, 337, 238.
22 Bukhari, *Tafsir, Ha.Mim, Al-Sajda (Fussilat)*, 1.
23 Abu Dawud, *Adab*, 49, 4896–97.
24 Abu Dawud, *Adab*, 7, 4800.
25 Muslim, *Iman*, 58.
26 Ibn al-Athir, *Al-Nihaya fi Gharib al-Hadith*, I, 470.
27 Tirmidhi, *Kiyama*, 23, Hadith no. 2457.
28 Muslim, *Hayd*, 13, 61.
29 Muslim, *Iman*, 12, 60.
30 Bukhari, *Adab*, 69; Muslim, *Birr*, 102–3/2606–7; Muwatta, *Kalam*, 16/2, 989; Abu Dawud, *Adab*, 88/4989; Tirmidhi, *Birr*, 46, 1972.
31 Bukhari, *Zakat*, 25; *Wakalat*, 16; *Ijara*, 1; Muslim, *Zakat*, 79, 1023; Abu Dawud, *Zakat*, 43, 1684; Nasai, *Zakat*, 66, 5, 79–80.
32 Abu Dawud, *Adab*, 80; Ibn Hanbal, *Musnad*, 3/447.
33 Ibn Hanbal, *Musnad*, 2/452.
34 Ibn Hanbal, *Musnad*, 3/198.
35 Muslim, *Iman*, 43.
36 Tirmidhi, *Kiyama*, 61, 2520; Nasai, *Ashriba*, 8, 327, 328.

37 Muslim, *Iman*, 62, 38,
38 Tirmidhi, *Birr*, 57, 1991,
39 Abu Dawud, *Adab*, 93, 5003; Tirmidhi, *Fitan*, 3, 2161,
40 Abu Dawud, *Adab*, 93, 5004,
41 Yazir, *Hak Dini Kur'an Dili*, VI, 4467–71.
42 Yazir, ibid.
43 Yazir, ibid., 1/236–42.
44 *Shirk* is the unforgivable wrong action of worshipping something or some-one other than God or associating something or someone as a partner with Him.
45 Ibn Hanbal, *Musnad*, V, 428.
46 Ibn Hanbal, *Musnad*, IV, 124.
47 Muslim, *Zuhd*, 46.
48 Muslim, *Imara*, 152.
49 Muslim, *Birr*, 166.
50 Ghazali, *Ihya al-Ulum al-Din*, 7/433–567.
51 Nursi, *Lem'alar, İkinci Lem'a*, 581.
52 Ibid., *Onbirinci Lem'a*, 609.
53 Ibid., *Kastamonu Lahikası*, 1639.
54 Ibid.
55 Ibid, *Ondokuzuncu Lem'a*, 660.
56 Gülen, *Kırık Testi*.
57 Ünal, *Fethullah Gülen ile Amerika'da Bir Ay*, "Riya, Riyayı Tanıma ve Ondan Kurtulma."
58 Tirmidhi, *Kıyama*, 61, 2522.
59 Tirmidhi, *Fitan*, 76, 2264.
60 Tirmidhi, *Dawat*, 66, 3474.
61 Tirmidhi, *Buyu*, 4, 1209; Ibn Maja, *Tijara*, 1, 2139.
62 Bukhari, *Istizan*, 46; Muslim, *Fadail al-Sahaba*, 145, 2482.
63 Tirmidhi, *Zuhd*, 61, 2412.
64 Tirmidhi, *Qiyama*, 51, 2502.
65 Tirmidhi, *Zuhd*, 11, 2217.
66 Bukhari, *Rikak*, 23; Muslim, *Zuhd*, 49, 2988; *Muwatta*, 4, 985; Tirmidhi, *Zuhd*, 10, 2315.
67 Tirmidhi, *Zuhd*, 63, 2414.
68 Tirmidhi, *Zuhd*, 62, 3413.
69 Muslim, *Ilm*, 7, 2670; Abu Dawud, *Sunna*, 6, 4609.
70 Tirmidhi, *Birr*, 58.

71 Abu Dawud, *Adab*, 7, 4800.

72 Bukhari, *Adab*, 60; Muslim, *Zuhd*, 52, 2990.

73 Muslim, *Birr*, 139, 2623; Muwatta, *Kalam*, 2/2, 989; Abu Dawud, *Adab*, 85, 4989.

74 *Majmuat al-Tafasir*, VI/327–329.

75 Muslim, *Iman*, 45, 170; Bukhari, *Adab*, 50; Muslim, *Iman*, 169, 105; Abu Dawud, *Adab*, 38, 4771; Tirmidhi, *Birr*, 79, 2027.

76 Abu Dawud, *Adab*, 40, 4874; Tirmidhi, *Birr*, 23, 1935; Muslim, *Birr*, 70, 2589.

77 Abu Dawud, *Adab*, 40, 4875; Tirmidhi, *Sifat al-Qiyama*, 52, 2503–4.

78 Abu Dawud, *Adab*, 41, 4883.

79 Abu Dawud, *Adab*, 60; Muslim, *Zuhd*, 52, 2990.

80 Ibn Manzur, *Lisan al-Arab*, 3/148.

81 Gülen, *Zaman* (daily newspaper), "Akademi", March 19, 2004.

82 Ghazali, *Ihya al-Ulum al-Din*, 3/425–6.

83 Yazir, *Hak Dini Kur'an Dili*, II, 1164.

84 Mawdudi, *Tafhim al-Qur'an*, 7/326.

85 Ibn Hanbal, *Musnad*, 3/166.

86 Tirmidhi, *Sifat al-Kiyama*, 57, 2512.

87 Bukhari, *Ilm*, 15; Muslim, *Salat al-Musafirin*, 268, 816.

88 Tirmidhi, *Salat*, 433; Nasai, *Bay'at*, 35.

89 Munawi, *Fayd al-Qadir*, 5/373; *Kanz al-Ummal*, 1, 146.

90 Muslim, *Salaam*, 40, 2186.

91 Nursi, *Mektubat*, 2, 471.

92 Abu Dawud, *Adab*, 44.

93 Nursi, *Mektubat*, 2, 471.

94 Ghazali, *Ihya al-Ulum al-Din*, 3/440–2.

95 Ibid., 3/445–6.

96 Gülen, *Zaman* (daily newspaper), "Akademi," March 19, 2004.

97 Bukhari, *Adab*, 57–58.

98 Ibn Manzur, *Lisan al-Arab*, 6/38.

99 Tirmidhi, *Birr*, 85.

100 Ibn Maja, *Sunan*, Vol. II, Hadith no. 2547.

101 Muslim, *Birr*, 70; Tirmidhi, *Birr*, 23.

102 Ibn Hanbal, *Musnad*, 6/461.

103 Bayhaqi, *Sunan al-Kubra*, 9/54–5; Ibn Hanbal, *Musnad*, 4/279; Haythami, *Majma al-Zawaid*, 7/108–111.

104 Qurtubi, *Al-Jamiu li-Ahqam al-Qur'an*, 16/316.

CHAPTER 4: PROMOTING GOOD CHARACTER IN SOCIAL LIFE

1   See 6:54, 7:46, 13:24, 16:32, 28:55, 39:73.

2   Bukhari, *Istizan*, 1.

3   Muslim, *Iman*, 22; Abu Dawud, *Salaam*, 1; Tirmidhi, *Istizan*, 43.

4   Tirmidhi, *Istizan*, 15.

5   Bukhari, *Istizan*, 27.

6   Abu Dawud, *Adab*, 153.

7   Bukhari, *Istizan*, 27; Tirmidhi, *Istizan*, 31/2730.

8   Tirmidhi, *Istizan*, 31/2731.

9   Muwatta, *Husn al-Khulq*, 16/2, 908.

10 Ibn Hanbal, *Musnad*, 5/163, 168.

11 Bukhari, *Istizan*, 28.

12 Ibn Maja, *Adab*, 21.

13 Tirmidhi, *Istizan*, 31; Ibn Hanbal, *Musnad*, 5/260; see also the Qur'an 4:86.

14 Malik, *Muwatta*, 47, 476.

15 Bukhari, *Iman*, 7.

16 Muslim, *Birr*, 8, 2560; Abu Dawud, *Adab*, 55.

17 Bukhari, *Adab*, 57.

18 Bukhari, *Wasaya*, 16; *Jihad*, 103; *Manaqib*, 23; *Manaqib al-Ansar*, 43; *Maghazi*, 3, 78; *Tafsir, Baraa*, 17–19; *Istizan*, 21; *Ayman*, 24; *Ahkam*, 53; Muslim, *Tawba*, 53, 2769; Tirmidhi, *Tafsir, Baraa*, 3101.

19 Muslim, *Birr*, 36; Muwatta, *Husn al-Khulq*, 17.

20 See Abu Dawud, *Adab*, 142; Tirmidhi, *Istizan*, 31; Ibn Maja, *Adab*, 15; Ibn Hanbal, *Musnad*, 4/289, 303.

21 Abu Dawud, *Adab*, 100, 5036; Tirmidhi, *Adab*, 5, 2745; Ibn Maja, *Adab*, 20, 3714.

22 Bukhari, *Adab*, 125, 128; *Bad al-Khalq*, 11; Muslim, *Zuhd*, 56, 2994; Abu Dawud, *Adab*, 97, 5028.

23 Abu Dawud, *Adab*, 98, 5029; Tirmidhi, *Adab*, 6, 2746.

24 Bukhari, *Adab*, 127; Muslim, *Zuhd*, 53, 2991; Abu Dawud, *Adab*, 102, 5039.

25 Bukhari, *Janaiz*, 2; Muslim, *Salaam*, 4–6.

26 Tirmidhi, *Birr*, 47.

27 Bukhari, *Adab*, 29.

28 Muslim, *Iman*, 73.

29 Ajluni, *Kashf al-Khafa*, 1/178.

30 Nasai, *Istiadha*, 44; Ibn Hanbal, *Musnad*, 2/344.

31 Bukhari, *Adab*, 28; Muslim, *Birr wa Sila wa Adab*, 140/2624–5.

32 Ibn Hanbal, *Musnad*, 1/55.

33 Tabarani, *Al-Mu'jam al-Kabir*, 1/232; Haysami, *Majma al-Zawaid*, 8/167.

34 Ibn Hanbal, *Musnad*, 2/33.

35 Muslim, *Birr wa Sila wa al-Adab*, 143, 2625.

36 Ajluni, *Kashf al-Khafa*, 1/72.

37 Ibrahim Hakki, *Marifetname*, 4/173.

38 Tirmidhi, *Birr*, 64.

39 Bukhari, *Adab*, 65.

40 Kandahlawi, quoted from the translation of *Hayat al-Sahaba*, ("The Prophet's Companions' Way of Life"), Vol. III, 1115.

41 Bukhari, *Adab*, 65.

42 Kandahlawi, ibid.

43 Bukhari, *Al-Adab al-Mufrad*, 1065.

44 Ibn Hanbal, *Musnad*, 4/189.

45 Bukhari, *Ashriba*, 19; Muslim, *Ashriba*, 127; Ibn Hanbal, *Musnad*, 1/284.

46 Bukhari, *At'ima*, 57, 34; *Buyu*, 21; *Mazalim*, 14; Muslim, *Ashriba*, 138, 2036; Tirmidhi, *Nikah*, 12, 1099.

47 Bukhari, *Nikah*, 71, 74; Muslim, *Nikah*, 103, 1429; Tirmidhi, *Nikah*, 11, 1098; Abu Dawud, *At'ima*, 1, 3736–39.

48 Bukhari, *Nikah*, 71, 74; Muslim, *Nikah*, 103, 1429; Tirmidhi, *Nikah*, 11, 1098; Abu Dawud, *At'ima*, 1, 3736–39.

49 Abu Dawud, *At'ima*, 9, 3756.

50 Ibn Maja, *At'ima*, 28; Ibn Hanbal, *Musnad*, 4/108.

51 Tirmidhi, *Adab*, 13, 2755.

52 Abu Dawud, *Adab*, 165, 5230.

53 Abu Dawud, *Adab*, 165, 5229; Tirmidhi, *Adab*, 13, 2756.

54 Abu Dawud, *Adab*, 24, 4844–45; Tirmidhi, *Adab*, 11, 2753.

55 Bukhari, *Istizan*, 45; Muslim, *Salaam*, 36, 2183; Muwatta, *Kalam*, 13/2, 988–89.

56 Bukhari, *Istizan*, 31; *Jum'a*, 20; Muslim, *Salaam*, 27, 2177; Tirmidhi, *Adab*, 9, 2750–51; Abu Dawud, *Adab*, 18.

57 Tirmidhi, *Adab*, 10, 2752.

58 Bukhari, *Janaiz*, 2; Muslim, *Libas*, 114.

59 Tirmidhi, *Adab*, 45; Nasai, *Janaiz*, 53.

60 Bukhari, *Jihad*, 171.

61 Bukhari, *Tawhid*, 31.

62 Muslim, *Birr*, 43.

63 Tirmidhi, *Janaiz*, 4; Abu Dawud, *Tibb*, 17.

64 Tirmidhi, *Tibb*, 32; Ibn Hanbal, *Sunan*, 1/239.

65 Bukhari, *Istidhan*, 29.

66 Ibn Hanbal, *Musnad*, 3/175.

67 Abu Dawud, *Janaiz*, 6.

68 Bukhari, *Tamanni*, 6; Muslim, *Dhikr*, 10, 13.

69 Abu Dawud, *Sunan*, 2/85.

70 Saba 34:30; A'raf 7:34; Hud 11:3.

71 Ibn Maja, *Janaiz*, 1.

72 Bukhari, *Istizan*, 29.

73 Tirmidhi, *Daawat*, 112; see also Baqara 2:201.

74 Bukhari, *Janaiz*, 69; Muslim, *Janaiz*, 57, 946; Abu Dawud, *Janaiz*, 45, 3168; Nasai, *Janaiz*, 54, 59; Tirmidhi, *Janaiz*, 49, 1040; Ibn Maja, *Janaiz*, 34, 1539.

75 Muwatta, *Janaiz*, 13/1, 226; Abu Dawud, *Janaiz*, 46, 3171.

76 See Al Imran 3:185; Anbiya 21:35; Ankabut 29:57.

77 Anbiya 21:8, 34.

78 Insan 76:2.

79 Ahzab 33:16.

80 Baqara 2:28, 281; Anbiya 21:35.

81 Ahzab 33:41; Fatir 35: 3.

82 Tirmidhi, *Janaiz*, 50, 1041.

83 Tirmidhi, *Janaiz*, 26, 1007.

84 Tirmidhi, *Janaiz*, 34, 1019.

85 Bukhari, *Janaiz*, 86; *Shahada*, 6; Muslim, *Janaiz*, 60, 949; Tirmidhi, *Janaiz*, 63, 1058.

86 Tirmidhi, *Qiyama*, 26; *Zuhd*, 4; Nasai, *Janaiz*, 3; Ibn Maja, *Zuhd*, 31.

87 Muslim, *Janaiz*, 105, 108; *Adahi*, 37; Abu Dawud, *Janaiz*, 75; Tirmidhi, *Janaiz*, 60; Nasai, *Janaiz*, 100–101.

88 Bukhari, *Wasaya*, 15.

89 Muslim, *Wasiyyah*, 14.

90 Ibn Maja, *Janaiz*, 47.

91 Nasif, *Al-Taj, al-Jami al-Usul*, II, 190.

92 Bukhari, *Sulh*, 11; *Jihad*, 72, 128; Muslim, *Zakat*, 56; *Musafirin*, 84; Abu Dawud, *Tatawwu*, 12; *Adab*, 160; Ibn Hanbal, *Musnad*, 2/316, 350, 4/423, 5/178.

BIBLIOGRAPHY

Abu Ghudda, Abdul Fattah, *Safahat min Sabr al-Ulama*, Beirut, 1987.

Ajluni, *Kashf al-Khafa*, Beirut: Dar al-Kutub al-Ilmi, 1988.

Azimabadi, Abu al-Tayyib Muhammad, *Awn al-Ma'bud*, Medina, 1968.

Bayhaki, *Sunan al-Kubra*, Beirut: Dar al-Maarif, undated.

Bilmen, Ömer Nasuhi, *Büyük İslam İlmihali*.

Ghazali, *Ihya al-Ulum al-Din*, Istanbul: Bedir Yayınları, 1975.

Gülen, M. Fethullah, *Kırık Testi*, Istanbul: Zaman Kitap, 2003.

------, *Prizma*, İzmir: Nil Yayınları, 2001.

------, *Sonsuz Nur*, İzmir: Nil Yayınları, 2001.

Ibn al-Athir, *Al-Nihaya fi Gharib al-Hadith*, Beirut: Dar al-Fikr, undated.

Ibn Hajar, *Fath al-Bari*, Cairo: Dar al-Rayyan Li al-Turas al-Arabi, 1986.

Haysami, *Majma al-Zawaid wa Manba al-Fawaid*, Cairo: Maktab al-Kudsi, undated.

Ibrahim Hakkı, *Marifetname*, Istanbul: Bahar Yayınevi, undated.

Jassas, *Ahkam al-Qur'an*, Beirut, 1335 AH.

Kadi, Nasafi, Hazin, Ibn Abbas, *Majma al-Tafasir*, Istanbul: Çağrı Yay. 1994.

El-Karahisari, Mustafa bin Şemseddin, *Ahter-i Kebir*, undated.

Ibn Kathir, *Al-Bidaya wa al-Nihaya*, Cairo: Dar al-Ihya al-Turas al-Arabi, 1968.

------, *Mukthasar Tafsir*, Beirut: Dar al-Qur'an al-Karim, Beirut, 1981.

Ibn Manzur, *Lisan al-Arab*, Beirut: Dar al-Sadr, 1993.

Mawdudi, Abu al-Ala, *Tafhim al-Qur'an*, Istanbul: İnsan Yayınları, 1988.

Mawlana Shibli, *Asr-ı Saadet*, (trns. O. Riza Dogrul), Istanbul, 1974.

Al-Mawsili, *Al-Ikhtiyar*, Istanbul: Yüksel Matbaası, 1973.

Munawi, *Fayd al-Qadir*, Beirut, Dar al-Ma'rifa, undated.

Al-Munziri, *Al-Targib wa al-Tarhib*, Cairo: Dar al-Ihya al-Turas al-Arabi, 1968.

Nasif, Mansur Ali, *Al-Taj al-Jami al-Usul*, Dar al-Ihya al-Turas al-Arabi, Beirut, 1961.

Nursi, Bediüzzaman Said, *Risale-i Nur Külliyatı*, Istanbul: Nesil Yayınları, 1996.

Qurtubi, *Al-Jami Li Ahkam al-Qur'an*, Cairo, 1967.

Qutb, Sayyid, *Fi Zilal al-Qur'an*, Cairo, 1986.

Ibn Sa'd, *Tabaqat al-Kubra*, Beirut: Dar al-Fikr, 1994.

Suyuti, *Jami al-Saghir*, Beirut: Dar al-Kutub al-Ilmiyya, 1990.

Türkiye Diyanet Vakfı *İslam Ansiklopedisi*, Istanbul: Güzel Sanatlar Matbaası, 1998.

Ünal, Ismail, *F. Gülen'le Amerika'da Bir Ay*, Istanbul: Işık Yayınları, 2001.

Yazır, Elmalılı Hamdi, *Hak Dini Kur'an Dili*, Istanbul: Eser Neşriyat, 1979.

INDEX

A

Aaron (Prophet), 94, 146

Abbas ibn Abdul Muttalib, xi

'Abdullah ibn Amr ibn al-As, 44, 49, 89, 124

'Abdullah ibn Busr, 158

'Abdullah ibn Ja'far, 62

'Abdullah ibn Mas'ud, 24, 74, 84, 88, 112, 124, 140, 155

'Abdullah ibn Qays, 154

'Abdullah ibn Rawaha, 69

'Abdullah ibn Shaddad, 35

'Abdullah ibn Ubayy, 69

'Abdullah ibn Umar, 61-62, 84, 112, 161, 164

Abdur Rahman ibn Awf, 75

Abdur Rahman ibn Sahl, 37

ablution, 55, 57, 59, 75, 78-79, 124

Abraham (Prophet), 88

Abu Abdur Rahman, 155

Abu al-Darda, 24-25, 155

Abu al-Hawra, 90

Abu Baddah al-Tujibi, 41

Abu Bakr, x, xvi, 43, 63, 80, 82, 169

Abu Dharr al-Ghifari, 23, 94, 151

Abu Hafs, 11

Abu Hurayra, 15-16, 26, 44, 79, 89-91, 102, 107, 111-112, 114, 116-117, 144-145, 149, 151-152, 173

'Abdullah ibn Abu Bakr, 80

Abu Jahl, 69, 94

Abu Musa al-Ash'ari, 37, 62, 88, 158

Abu Said al-Khudri, 71, 78, 108, 125, 158

Abu Shuayb, 160-161

Abu Umama, 55, 61, 163

Abu Usayd Malik ibn Rabi'a al-Saidi, 44

Abu Yahya, 37

Abu Yusuf, 170

adab, ix-xv, xvii, xix, 3-4, 10-12, 15-17, 23, 26, 28, 31, 37, 41-42, 53, 61, 69, 85-86, 93, 137, 158, 161-162, 173; in practice, 3-4; of asking for permission, 53; of knowledge, 23; of learning, 28; of sitting in gatherings, 26; of teaching, 31; toward parents, 41

adab al-muasharat, 10, 17

Al-Adab al-Mufrad, 15, 189

Adam (Prophet), 137

adhan (call to prayer), 139

advice, 24, 79, 127, 145-148, 152, 154; giving of, 148

Aisha bint Abu Bakr, x, 57, 74, 85, 94, 116, 150, 165

akhlaq, 3, 67, 71, 73, 131

Ali ibn Abu Talib, 24, 28-29, 62, 90